ADAMS MEDIA
New York London Toronto Sydney New Delhi

adamsmedia
Adams Media
An Imprint of Simon & Schuster, Inc.
100 Technology Center Drive
Stoughton, Massachusetts 02072



First Adams Media trade paperback edition April 2023



Interior design, illustrations, and hand lettering by Priscilla Yuen

Manufactured in the United States of America

1 2023

Library of Congress Cataloging-in-Publication Data
Names: Smit, Jana Louise, author.
Title: How to kill an earworm / Jana Louise Smit.
Description: Stoughton, Massachusetts: Adams Media, 2023. |
Includes bibliographical references.
Identifiers: LCCN 2022049293 |
ISBN 9781507220283 (pb) |
ISBN 9781507220290 (ebook)
Subjects: LCSH: Psychology--Popular works. | Psychology--Miscellanea.
Classification: LCC BF145 .S5626 2023 |
DDC 150--dc23/eng/20221212
LC record available at
https://lccn.loc.gov/2022049293

ISBN 978-1-5072-2028-3
ISBN 978-1-5072-2029-0 (ebook)

# CONTENTS

# INTRODUCTION

**Did you know...**

- Evolutionary psychology can explain why introverted cave people lived longer.
- Advertisers capitalize on social psychology to trick you into Black Friday sales.
- Sarcasm can be an indicator of whether the brain is healthy or not.

If these questions kick-started your thirst for psychological knowledge, you've come to the right place. Throughout this book, you'll find more than five hundred psychology facts that will teach you more than you ever thought you'd know about the human mind. Broken up by the different branches of psychology, each chapter explores why humans are so infinitely complex, how brains change (or stay the same) over generations, and, more specifically, why people behave in the ways that they do.

- Your brain's growth from barely functioning baby to mostly functioning adult as studied in Developmental Psychology.
- Biopsychology and Behavioral Psychology, or why people act in the ways they do.
- How your emotions dictate who you are, as discussed in Personality Psychology.
- Forensic and Abnormal Psychologies, which primarily delve into the minds of criminals.
- And more!

To keep things interesting, this book provides several different ways for you to learn fun, new facts. The surprising rapid oddities and short trivia facts are quick and easy to digest. The longer trivia facts are perfect if you want an in-depth explanation. More in the mood for a challenge? Tackle a psych test to assess your knowledge of the human mind, but don't forget to test your fellow trivia fans too! You'll find the answers for each quiz in the Appendix at the back of the book.

So whether you're looking to learn more about a specific branch of psychology, want to know more about how others (including those long-dead) have influenced your brain, or just want to know how to finally rid yourself of that ridiculous earworm, read on!

# CHAPTER 1

# THE HISTORY OF PSYCHOLOGY:

## AN EXPLORATION OF PSYCHOLOGY FROM OUR ANCIENT ANCESTORS TO NEW FRONTIERS

You might have your Aunt Maggie's headstrong nature or your grandfather's lack of a sense of direction, but your heritage does not stop there. It goes way, way back. Indeed, your prehistoric ancestors still influence some of your worst fears and strongest instincts. How *do* dinosaur-like behaviors dwell in you?

The answer is simple: evolutionary psychology! This branch offers intriguing insights into the part of the mind that refuses to abandon the past. These primitive instincts kept your ancestors alive, and they are still intent on keeping you safe from predators (and jealous tribe members!).

Cave people not your thing? Be prepared to "visit" different eras: Gaze into the minds of the ancient Egyptians and dive into the darkly magnetic psychology of the Middle Ages. The golden oldies explored in this chapter will make you a hit at your next history trivia night! Evolution is still happening on a daily basis; that's why this chapter ponders the psychological future too. Explore a stellar collection of space trivia, including a lot of strange occurrences that happen to astronauts and how the human mind might deal with future space colonization. Finally, enjoy all the fun facts about how your brain is already responding to current technology! You might never look at your smartphone the same again....

Throughout this chapter, you're invited to get your brain in gear and witness the remarkable adaptability of human cognition throughout the ages. So if you're wondering why the childhood monster that lived in your closet was real (to a degree), how space can turn astronauts a little dumb, or when fear can trigger a reaction that's surprisingly similar to a possum playing dead, then hold on to your hat: You're about to get a stiff dose of pre- and post-historic trivia!

## HIPPOCRATES REALLY DIDN'T GET PSYCHOLOGY

Your personality is a unique blend of genetics and changes brought on by life experiences. But ancient Greek thinkers believed that people gained their personalities from bodily fluids. Even famous Greek physicians Hippocrates and Galen believed that these "humors" were responsible for human behavior and that certain illnesses were also linked to each. According to the good doctors, ***four humors ruled the mind and body: blood, phlegm, black bile, and yellow bile***.

If you were lucky, you had an excess of blood, which led to a cheerful disposition, or a "sanguine" mood. If the body had mostly phlegm, the person was calm or "phlegmatic." Not all the humors were candy-coated, though. The so-called black bile was the monster behind depression, while too much yellow bile caused angry outbursts. These were called "melancholic" and "choleric" temperaments, respectively.

To treat that violent fishmonger or the sad customer who just wanted to buy hake without getting yelled at, physicians tried to balance the humors. Most treatments relied on observing the patient and changing their diet. ***More drastic cases were purged in less-than-delightful ways.*** These methods included bloodletting and laxatives.

### RAPID ODDITY

The belief that **humors** (a.k.a. bodily fluids) caused sickness and smiles alike persisted for nearly two thousand years.

## RAPID ODDITY

Plato believed the **soul had three parts**, which reflected society's rationality, desires, and emotions.

### SPACE STUPIDITY IS REAL

Being an astronaut comes with public admiration, a gold star for being smart, and loads to tell the grandkids one day. But then there's also the unflattering "***space stupids***." In medical terms, it's called "sopite syndrome," a subtle form of motion sickness. On Earth, researchers believe it might be behind the drowsiness that babies feel when they are being rocked. But in space, sopite syndrome is less kind to astronauts who experience ***symptoms like disorientation, mental fog, and lethargy***. The triggers are not fully understood, making this condition an unpredictable risk during missions.

**PSYCH TEST Not Feeling the Space Joy**

Floating around in space can be mentally taxing. What is the most common psychological problem faced by astronauts?

- a. Depression and anxiety.
- b. Frustration.
- c. Claustrophobia or feeling confined.
- d. Homesickness.

**Nomophobia** is the fear of losing your cell phone—or having to go somewhere without it.

## HUMANS PLAY DEAD TOO

Plenty of animals play dead. Opossums, beetles, some ducks, and, yes, even people. Sure enough, when the right things go wrong, humans experience a form of freezing. It's similar to animals in danger pretending to be dead, but the difference is that humans do this involuntarily. When faced with a dire situation where neither fight nor flight is possible, ***the primitive brain takes over and removes your ability to move***. Researchers believe this might be a last-ditch attempt to survive. By staying absolutely still, the threat—whatever it is—might get bored and leave.

### RAPID ODDITY

The English word "psychology" comes from the Greek ***psyche* and *logia***, meaning "study of the mind."

## AND THE INVENTOR OF THE WORD "PSYCHOLOGY" IS...

Put your mouth guard in for this one: When it comes to naming the first person who penned the word "psychology," experts are still taking swipes at each other. But whoever came up with the term, ***its roots might reach as far back as the 1500s***. During this time, a friend of Croatian poet Marko Marulić created a list of his works, and among the titles was *Psichiologia de ratione animae humanae*, a book published around 1524. Another contender is Philipp Melanchthon, a German writer who passed away in 1560.

## RAPID ODDITY

In 2016, a man **adored his cell phone** so much that he married it in Las Vegas.

**PSYCH TEST** How to Show Ancient Regret

Which nonverbal cue might have evolved to show others that an embarrassing social scene was not meant as a threat?

a. Blushing.
b. Lowering of the eyes.
c. Turning away.
d. Smiling.

## YOUR STONE AGE BRAIN HATES CHANGE

Evolutionary psychologists believe that ***there is a cave person in all of us*** and that this "leftover" resists change at all costs—even if it's just by giving you a persistent feeling of worry! Because back in the day, leaving the comfort of a well-stocked cave meant encountering hostile tribes and/or hungry predators, or falling down a hole. Considering that humans lived the majority of their evolutionary existence in caves with a scary view, it's not surprising that they are hardwired today to feel threatened by anything that upsets the apple cart.

## RAPID ODDITY

Victorian society became **obsessed with death**, partly because Queen Victoria kept mourning her husband.

## A TERRIBLE MEDIEVAL ILLNESS CALLED...LOVE?

Medieval doctors had a tough time with a persistent disease: ***love-sick suitors***. Many people came down with fuzzy feelings and, when rejected by the object of their affection, experienced severe melancholy and sadness.

Not quite understanding how love worked, most physicians believed that the emotions or hurt feelings had nothing to do with their patients' moping. ***Nope, you had too much black bile floating around inside your body!*** This led to a cold constitution, which, in turn, was thought to be responsible for melancholy. Suffering the aftereffects of a romantic rejection was viewed as a genuine physical illness and was treated as such, with the main focus on rebalancing the four humors (bodily fluids) in the body.

Instead of telling someone, "Hey, there's plenty of fish in the sea," doctors prescribed a couple of things that were surprisingly helpful for the time. ***Lovesick individuals were told to eat well, stay calm, roam in the garden, and experience more greenery and sunlight.*** They were also prescribed bed rest. Unfortunately, some medieval lovers were also purged of their emotional pain with useless antidotes for black bile...you guessed it: bloodletting and laxatives.

**PSYCH TEST** Name This Common Fear!

What is technophobia?

a. The fear of any technology.
b. The fear or dislike of advanced technology.
c. A specific fear of computers.
d. The fear of damaging expensive equipment.

## MARS MIGHT STEAL YOUR MARBLES

The mental health of future Martians is not looking rosy. The first colonists will probably face a one-way trip, and, a few weeks in, some might regret their decision. ***The shock of being stuck on a distant planet, away from family and familiar sights, can lead to an unprecedented mental illness.*** Should someone suffer a psychotic episode, the other pioneers will have to deal with the situation themselves. Despite all the planning to conquer other worlds, the Martian Police Department is probably not going to be ready in time to join the first colonists.

## THE TRUTH ABOUT THE MONSTER UNDER THE BED

At one point, most kids are convinced that there is a monster sitting in the closet or hiding under their bed. Even when Mom or Dad opens the closet and says, "See, there's nothing there," the unease remains. As an adult, you know the truth: There is no hairy horror lurking under the springs, just waiting to grab the nearest human ankle. But why are kids so independently persistent with this belief?

Evolutionary scientists theorize that kids are experiencing a ***modern version of when ancient ancestors feared unseen predators in the dark***. Indeed, this nocturnal awareness was an essential tool developed to survive what was often a brutal existence.

These days, kids might live in secure houses and might not particularly fear any predators. But this worry has kept humans alive for countless generations, and so it remains. When night falls, youngsters respond to an echo telling them to be extra careful of "something." Instead of fearing rival tribes or a cave bear, kids today draw on books and popular media to populate the dark with monsters and ghosts.

## RAPID ODDITY

**Phubbing**, or "phone snubbing," happens when someone ignores you in favor of their cell phone.

## GAMING EATS YOUR BRAIN

In a 2014 German research study, scientists wheeled gamers into an MRI room and scanned their heads. They also recruited people who didn't normally play computer games and asked them to engage in either Super Mario or first-person shooter games. This second group was allowed to bond with the famous plumber or shoot the living daylights out of the enemy for about ten weeks. Then their brains were also scanned.

The results revealed something interesting. The hippocampus is the brain region that is linked to memory, learning, stress management, navigation, and spatial awareness. This piece of gray matter shrunk in the volunteers who played shooting games. The people who guided Mario on his noble quest to save a princess experienced the exact opposite: Their hippocampi grew larger.

So, is this karma? You shoot imaginary targets' brains out, so you lose your own noodle? Not quite. ***The researchers suggested that the on-screen navigational systems of shooting games are to blame.*** The cues allow players to instantly orientate themselves, so there's no need to draw on the hippocampus for spatial and navigational information. Too many hours of this, and...hello, atrophy.

## STOCKHOLM SYNDROME IS SERIOUSLY ANCIENT

In 1973, several people were taken hostage in a bank in Stockholm, Sweden. When they were freed, the world was perplexed by their behavior. ***The bank employees begged police not to harm their captors and even cried when the criminals were arrested.*** The hostages were clearly fond of the men who had held them captive in the bank's vault for almost a week.

Most people who watched the drama unfold in the seventies, and those who heard the story in later years, mostly share the same conviction—that it's a rare occurrence and any hostage who loves their captor should be wheeled into the psych ward. But a recent study by Michelle Scalise Sugiyama of the University of Oregon suggested that, while the term "Stockholm syndrome" was coined only months after the bank heist, ***humans have relied on this bizarre bond for thousands of years to survive abduction, captivity, and tribal violence***. Lethal raids often brought home captives, and integrating oneself with the enemy greatly reduced the risk of being killed.

Stockholm syndrome is still going strong. For example, it's a common coping mechanism in abusive relationships, which makes it even harder for the victims to free themselves.

### PSYCH TEST Humanoids Creep Us Out

Which effect, when triggered by the movements of fake humanoids like robots, dolls, and even monkeys, often leaves people with a sense of unease?

- **a.** Robot phobia.
- **b.** The Abilene paradox.
- **c.** The uncanny valley effect.
- **d.** The contrast effect.

## WANT TO SURVIVE AS A HUNTER-GATHERER? HUG SOMEONE

In evolutionary biology, giving someone a good squeeze has a purpose. A very important purpose. When you hug a loved one, your brain rewards you with a cocktail of feel-good hormones, including oxytocin and serotonin. ***These magic ingredients are responsible for the close-knit feelings*** that strengthen bonds between life partners, parents and babies, and friends. In ancient times, these relationships could make or break a community's ability to survive, thus making the hug so much more than just a display of affection.

### RAPID ODDITY

Clinical depression was first described in the **Ebers Papyrus**, an Egyptian document from 1500 B.C.

## TECHNOLOGY SPEEDS UP TIME

Every year, life seems to shoot by faster than we'd like. Especially as we grow older! This phenomenon is a mystery, but scientists have a suspect in cuffs: your smartphone. The accused is also in cahoots with your favorite computer games, online work platforms, and basically any technology that grips your attention. ***Mentally disappearing into a phone or laptop can make you underestimate how much time has passed.*** If every day is a screen-fest, then it could be the reason why your calendar is flipping over new months like crazy.

**PSYCH TEST Why Doomscrolling Keeps You Hooked**

Doomscrolling refers to spending an excessive amount of time reading bad news online. Why can it be so hard to stop once you start doomscrolling?

a. Fear and uncertainty drive people to seek answers.
b. It's kind of entertaining.
c. Other people's misery makes you feel safer.
d. It feels responsible to stay on top of current news events.

## STORYTELLING WAS NEVER ABOUT ESCAPISM

When scientists realized that most adults spend a sizeable chunk of their day watching or reading stories, they wondered if there was an evolutionary purpose to this need to escape into a fictional world. But when they looked at the roots of storytelling, a surprising theory was born. Fiction is not really about escaping that soul-crushing job or, back in the day, a difficult existence as a hunter-gatherer. It's social glue—with a focus on how to live better.

***As ancient tribes became larger, they had to avoid conflict within the group, and tales played an important role in keeping the peace.*** A lot of stories revolved around serving the community, solving problems together, and understanding others. The undesirability of tyrants was also highlighted. Groups spending time together listening to stories probably also bonded more. But does this ancient tool of positive training persist today?

Scans have shown that stories activate the brain's emotional and social centers, which could explain why bookworms tend to have more empathy for others. Community-oriented themes have also never lost their appeal. People still root for characters who fight evil and always do the right thing.

**PSYCH TEST** **A Quirky Brain Reaction to Space**

Astronauts have to deal with a lot of physical challenges. But which unexpected mental effect is frequently reported by astronauts in space?

a. Feeling bored.
b. Claustrophobia.
c. Hallucinations.
d. Vertigo.

## PTSD MIGHT'VE SPAWNED SALEM'S WITCH TRIALS

Most people who develop post-traumatic stress disorder (PTSD) don't upset their hometown to the point where they execute nineteen people. But this disorder could explain why several girls in Salem, Massachusetts, experienced strange "fits" in 1692. At the time, the cause was believed to be witchcraft. The rest is gallows history. Many modern experts have tried to diagnose the girls' mysterious, seemingly contagious fits. While some suspect they faked it, there's a chance that they suffered from PTSD-related groupthink (most of the girls were war refugees). ***They might've developed "conversion disorder," whereby mental anguish causes twitching, garbled speech, and trances.***

## RAPID ODDITY

Ancient Egyptians coveted their pets because they believed the **animals were gifts from the gods**.

## STARING ROBOTS ARE AWKWARD

A hard stare from somebody can be very alarming. Researchers wanted to test whether this visceral response to a glare also counted for robots. For this experiment, they chose the perfect bot for the job. The iCub's nose and mouth were almost nonexistent, but it had a pair of eyes so large, you couldn't miss them if you tried.

Each participant played a computer game with the humanoid iCub. At certain times, they had to look at the robot's eyes before making a decision about their next move. Amazingly (or perhaps disturbingly), ***the bot's stare slowed down their ability to decide***. When the iCub averted its eyes, response times became quicker.

Since the participants wore EEG hoodies, the scientists could watch the brain's response to being ogled by a robot. Interestingly, it treated the iCub as a living thing. The same attentional processes that arise when you focus on a person also kicked into action when the volunteers locked eyes with the iCub. ***Ignoring the bug-eyed bot also required mental effort, and this distraction delayed their decisions.***

## THE CLOUD IS YOUR EXTERNAL BRAIN

When the software firm Kaspersky Lab ran a survey, the goal was to understand how many people store their information online and how this affects the brain. ***Over 90 percent of those who responded admitted that they rely on the Cloud as an extra brain.*** This is Star Trek–level cool and everything, but the scientists also discovered that when you dump information into the Internet instead of the brain, it can lead to "digital amnesia." In other words, your memory muscle gets lazy and hampers your ability to remember things.

## RAPID ODDITY

**Cyberpsychology** studies the positive and negative impacts of online technology on mental health.

## ROBOTS AND SNAKES—WORSE THAN DEATH?

In 2015, researchers released the Survey of American Fears, designed to get people to (willingly) confess their innermost phobias. The results showed that ***tech jitters were alive and well***. Participants were most concerned about cybercrime and the unauthorized tracking of personal data. But perhaps the most interesting discovery was that the fear of death, which was roughly in the middle of the list, ranked lower than robots and even reptiles.

### PSYCH TEST Why Plague Physicians Looked So Freaky

In seventeenth-century Europe, plague doctors wore the now-infamous outfits that made them look like birds. Select the psychological reasoning behind their beaked masks.

- **a.** The ominous look kept infected people at bay.
- **b.** It made doctors more recognizable, especially in chaotic situations.
- **c.** The demonic appearance reminded victims that the plague was God's punishment.
- **d.** The mask's shape was thought to protect against infection.

### THE ANCIENTS OUTSOURCED THEIR GRIEF

In some ancient cultures, ***an open display of emotions was a no-no***. A weepy Roman man, in particular, was seen as a disgrace to everything with testosterone. This made things a bit awkward at funerals. After all, one could not stand there with a stony face and not look like a jerk. Then someone had the idea of ***hiring professional mourners to turn on the waterworks for them***. This solution did not just happen in Rome; it also popped up in South Africa, Egypt, China, and the Middle East.

**PSYCH TEST** **The Secret to Defeating an Egyptian Army**

In an early example of psychological warfare, the Persians won a battle against the ancient Egyptians by using cats as shields. Why did this work?

a. The Egyptians retreated, believing the animals were diseased.
b. Ancient Egyptian culture forbade the killing of cats.
c. The Egyptian army viewed cats as evil spirits.
d. The cats were taken from sacred temples, so the Egyptians yielded.

**RAPID ODDITY**

Our **warlike mindset** is ancient. Evidence shows that humans fought with Neanderthals for one hundred thousand years.

**PSYCH TEST** **If You're Ancient and You Know It...**

Clap your hands! Do you know which ancestral motive might've hardwired humans to use hand-clapping as a form of communication?

**a.** The lack of sophisticated speech.
**b.** To show both positive and negative emotions.
**c.** To communicate with sound over great distances.
**d.** A clapping group feels unified.

## HOW AN ANCIENT HEX BECAME A MODERN DIAGNOSIS

The symptoms of post-traumatic stress disorder (PTSD) were described three thousand years ago. Combatants in ancient Mesopotamia showed classic signs like nightmares, flashbacks, and depression. ***Back then, people assumed the soldiers were hexed by ghosts.*** Things didn't look up in modern times. During the First World War, soldiers suffered shell shock, which physicians linked to trauma, but their voices were drowned out by the popular belief that shell shock was plain cowardice. Soldiers from the Second World War and the Vietnam War faced similar ignorance. ***It wasn't until 1980 that PTSD became a formal diagnosis.***

## RAPID ODDITY

**Astronauts are kept happy** with enough family time, relaxation, privacy, and an understanding ground team.

## RAPID ODDITY

People share more angry posts than happy or sad ones, making **anger** one of the most viral online emotions.

### THE AMAZING PSYCHOLOGY OF EMOJIS

Whether it's a thumbs-up or a barf face, millions of emojis light up conversations every day. This didn't escape the notice of researchers, who jumped at the chance to discover what emojis mean to people emotionally and neurologically. The results showed that, consciously, you consider them as cute extras but nothing more. On the other hand, the brain engages with them on a much deeper level.

With or without your awareness, emojis are treated like real emotions, and, curiously, ***the main motivation for using them is to establish a positive vibe in conversations***. Indeed, most people send more grins or hearts than negative symbols.

Emoji psychology doesn't end with the person who sends them. It also helps those at the receiving end. In the "real world," cues gleaned from body language are important for effective human conversation, but they are absent during texting. ***Emojis could be an attempt to simulate what's missing***—and thus far, they're serving us very well! Both emojis and stickers can reveal emotional information about the sender, giving the other person a sense of how to respond.

**PSYCH TEST** **Why Tech and Kids Don't Always Mix**

Technology keeps children entertained and also provides them with better educational tools. But what are the main drawbacks of too much screen time for kids?

**a.** They stay up too late and become sleep-deprived.
**b.** Eye strain, irritability, and isolation.
**c.** They become addicted to entertainment.
**d.** Reduced social skills, risk of depression, and obesity.

## HUNTER-GATHERERS COULD BE PLAYFUL TOO

People can't exactly do a live study of the hunter-gatherers who lived when everyone on the planet had to pick berries and hunt animals to survive. But to understand the past, especially how people interacted with each other during this period, researchers don't have to rely solely on guesswork. Some hunter-gatherer tribes alive today allowed outsiders to study them—and this led to a surprising discovery.

Most people view such tribes as less advanced and thus prone to an unforgiving, even violent hierarchy. But some researchers, including Richard Lee in 1988, who studied several current hunter-gatherer communities, ***discovered that these people are actually, in their own words, "fiercely egalitarian."*** This means that every member of the tribe is considered equal, and any person who tries to dominate another is ostracized or threatened with expulsion from the group.

***Interestingly, the studies also found that the tribes work hard to keep their own instincts for dominance under control.*** Their societies are not naturally equal. However, because they understand the value of equality, they suppress aggression with playfulness. Their children play a lot, and the adults approach life in a fun mood. Even when they scold someone, they'll use humor before becoming more serious.

## A POCKETKNIFE BONDED OUR ANCESTORS

Once upon a time, people trooped out of Africa and spread across the world. Researchers believe that a key component to this successful migration was the ability to work together—and not just with one's own tribe. ***Those who learned to cooperate with other groups could also count on their allies for supplies and assistance in times of trouble.***

One discovery proved that ancient humans didn't constantly threaten their neighbors with a brutal mindset. Ironically, it was a weapon that revealed the existence of a remarkable social connectivity sixty-five thousand years ago in Southern Africa—long before people left Africa for the first time.

The tool in question was a "pocketknife," a small, knapped stone that was multifunctional. Used as a hand tool for cutting and cleaning, it could also be fixed to handles and shafts to produce axes and arrows. Archaeologists continue to find these tools across Southern Africa, and ***their near-identical design suggests that different groups, who were all connected to this vast social network, either traded them or shared the knowledge of how to make the tools.***

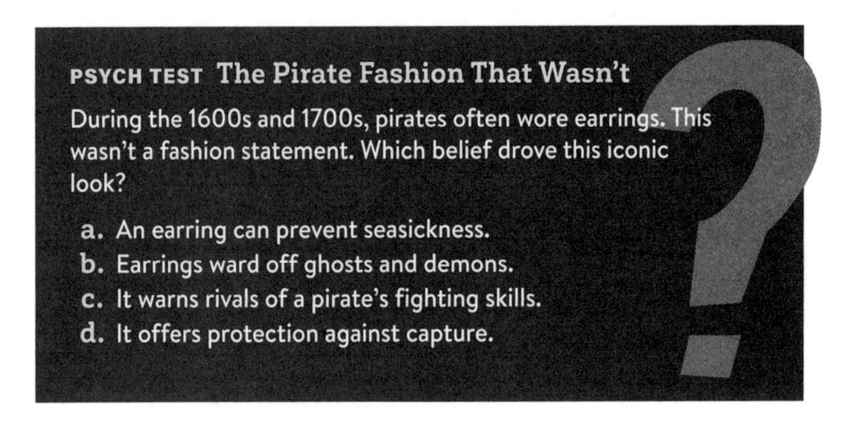

**PSYCH TEST** The Pirate Fashion That Wasn't

During the 1600s and 1700s, pirates often wore earrings. This wasn't a fashion statement. Which belief drove this iconic look?

a. An earring can prevent seasickness.
b. Earrings ward off ghosts and demons.
c. It warns rivals of a pirate's fighting skills.
d. It offers protection against capture.

## RAPID ODDITY

Native Amazonians' preindustrial lifestyle seems to **prevent dementia** (1 percent rate compared to America's 11 percent).

## CYBORG MOVIES MESS WITH BIONICS

Bionic limbs are a marvel. They use signals from a person's muscles, nerves, or brain to move seamlessly. But scientists in Germany found that, while such technology improves the lives of amputees, it does nothing to spare them from a new brand of stereotyping. In general, those with disabilities are viewed as friendly but incompetent. On the other hand, ***those with bionic prosthetics are viewed as more competent than able-bodied people—but also as less friendly***. Researchers fear that Hollywood-influenced portrayals of cyborgs might be responsible for this perception.

### PSYCH TEST When Martians Diss Mission Control

Space travelers are among the most disciplined professionals in existence. But some warn that future Mars colonists could revolt against Earth. Why?

a. The colonists will fall apart mentally.
b. A growing sense of independence.
c. They will blame Earth for their problems.
d. It's inevitable that one person will cause a mutiny.

In ancient Babylon, anxiety was believed to be **caused by demons or angry gods** and required priestly intervention.

**PSYCH TEST** **The Biological Roots of Monsters**

During the 1800s, Europeans believed that vampires and werewolves roamed free and attacked people. Which misunderstood illness could be behind the myths?

a. Rabies.
b. Mental illness.
c. Bubonic plague.
d. Leprosy.

## THIS OLD FEAR GIVES BUSINESSES A BLOODY NOSE

When the number thirteen lands on a Friday, people don't like it. Hard-core believers in bad luck tackle the next twenty-four hours as if it's an ordeal to survive, but ***this dread isn't a recent development in human history***. According to historians, it started either with Judas (the thirteenth person at the Last Supper) or the wholesale slaughter of the Knights Templar on Friday the thirteenth, 1307. Either way, so many people still refuse to do business on this day that it costs the US up to $900 million in losses every time!

## RAPID ODDITY

In 2015, Japanese mall robots had to be programmed to **run away** from abusive kids.

## A MYSTERIOUS HABIT THAT IS HERE TO STAY

Ever rapped your knuckles on wood? If so, you've partaken in an old, mysterious tradition! Researchers disagree over its origins and real meaning but most people don't care about who invented the habit. They just knock on wood for luck. Some historians believe it hails from pagan times when people believed in tree spirits. Another theory holds a children's game responsible. In the nineteenth century, kids playing tag were "safe" whenever they touched wood. Whatever its origin, ***this superstition is surprisingly global and deeply rooted, even among those who aren't superstitious***.

## FEED YOUR BRAIN THIS MUSIC

These days, binaural beats are freely available online. You can listen to them on *YouTube* or download the files on your phone from audio sites. But what exactly are they, and how do these beats influence the brain? In short, when you listen to binaural beats, two different frequencies are being played—one in each ear. ***Your brain then gives you a third, different frequency.***

For example, the left headphone is playing a frequency of 132 hertz (Hz), and the right is thumping away at 121 Hz. Your brain synchronizes the difference, which, in this case, is 11 Hz, and that's what you'll hear, as well as the two original beats.

According to an article in *NeuroHealth*, ***binaural beats might boost the brain and soothe the mind***, depending on which trippy tune you're listening to. Beats in the delta range (1–4 Hz) and theta range (4–8 Hz) are linked to better sleep, relaxation, meditation, and creativity. The alpha spectrum (8–13 Hz) offers the same benefits and increased positivity. Frequencies from 13–40 Hz are associated with enhanced learning, memory, and alertness.

**PSYCH TEST** **Why Flying Makes You Cry**

The advent of aviation beneficially changed the way people travel forever. But what factor, besides the fear of flying, makes passengers more likely to cry?

a. The cabin fever gets to be too much.
b. A mix of boredom and frustration.
c. Reduced oxygen in the bloodstream.
d. Leaving loved ones behind.

## ROBO-POOCH TO THE RESCUE

Therapy dogs rock. Whenever they come into hospitals and retirement homes, these fluff wonders uplift the sick and lonely almost instantly. But some patients cannot come into contact with animals due to medical concerns or a sterile environment. The dogs can also experience stress, especially in unfamiliar places and around young kids. A 2021 study reported in the *International Journal of Social Robotics* gathered together schoolchildren, live therapy dogs, and a robot to come up with an alternative that made everyone happy: robot therapy pets. ***The kids reported that they preferred the real dogs, but they spent more time with and admitted they had more fun with the robot.***

## RAPID ODDITY

If babies were born in space, they would risk developing such **brittle skeletons** that Earth's gravity would probably break their bones.

**PSYCH TEST Meet Virtual Reality's Best Mental Perks**

Gamers can experience negative consequences when playing too many video games. But how can interactive VR (virtual reality) be beneficial for a user's mental well-being?

a. It is a fun way to escape.
b. Players release frustration and violence in a healthy way.
c. It promotes commitment, physical activity, motivation, and stress release.
d. It encourages creativity, quick reflexes, and fear control.

## SOME FITNESS TRACKERS ARE TYRANTS

There's no denying the usefulness of fitness trackers. You can check the progress of your daily goals, heart rate, blood pressure, and calories burned. Most people have a healthy relationship with their wristbands, but some fall prey to their trackers in a way that has sports psychologists concerned. ***According to research, when someone becomes obsessed with the data, things go wrong.*** Exercise becomes less enjoyable, they fret over every target, motivation swirls down the drain, and, perhaps the worst of all, any physical activity that is not tracked doesn't "count."

**RAPID ODDITY**

In 2021, a surgeon visited NASA's International Space Station **as a hologram** and gave astronauts real-time consultations.

## RAPID ODDITY

**Ancient Romans believed seizures were a sign of being possessed by a divine being.**

## ALL BOW BEFORE THE CHICKEN

Sometimes, people don't think like their ancestors at all. One example is the humble chicken. In 500 B.C., the birds were such a novelty in central Europe that people revered and collected them. ***To eat a chicken back then would be like ordering a swan-mayo sandwich today.*** It just wasn't done. But eventually, the chicken went from a pedestal to the plate. Archaeologists aren't sure why this happened, but it appears that during the first century C.E., Roman-controlled Britain got over its holy hens and started chowing down on chicken platters.

### PSYCH TEST AI Takeover? Not So Much

The rapid evolution of artificial intelligence is something that made Stephen Hawking nervous. Despite his prediction that AI would end humanity, why is this unlikely?

- **a.** AI cannot become sentient, even when it appears to be.
- **b.** Robots always follow human orders.
- **c.** All AI is programmed to be friendly.
- **d.** Scientists have anti-takeover countermeasures in place.

## THE SOUL MIGHT BE THE OLDEST COMFORT

Souls have been saved (or damned) for centuries. In more ancient cultures, souls even went on complicated journeys through the underworld. ***This concept, that a fragment of yourself can survive the physical body, might be older than most religions.***

According to the experts, the idea of a soul likely arose when humans developed both the language to articulate the concept and the ability to think beyond the basics of day-to-day survival. If they had to choose a time, researchers estimate that the soul first appeared two hundred thousand years ago, when humanity experienced a cultural surge that was rich in art, religion, and fashion.

But what might've triggered this notion? That there's a part of us all that's both divine and immortal? ***Some speculate that the harsh reality of death triggered a self-soothing reaction and the soul was invented to shatter the permanence of mortality.*** Similar to other ancient ideas, one cannot truly pinpoint when the soul became a thing. However, it remains ingrained in the human psyche, even in those who are not particularly religious.

## HUG A ROBOT TO BOOST YOUR BUSINESS

For decades now, robots have punched their workday cards alongside their human colleagues. Since robots are here to stay, the University of Michigan wanted to answer an important question. Humans can bond with smartphones and cars, but can they also befriend robots at work? And would this improve the performance of a team containing both people and machines? After testing such mixed groups, ***the researchers concluded that human emotions played a role in effective cooperation***. Those who felt affection for their robotic teammates were consistently on the teams that performed better.

## IS MUSIC USELESS...?

In evolutionary science, a spandrel is a useless by-product of a useful trait. In recent times, psychologist Steven Pinker claimed that music was a spandrel of language development, and the scientific world blew up. The debate and studies that followed showed that calling music a useless spinoff might've been a little premature.

When researchers looked at how the brain responds to singing, especially in groups and between mothers and babies, there was such a positive response that one cannot imagine that singing, which is considered a form of music, is just a happy accident.

The exact reason why our ancestors first became enamored with banging on a drum or chanting together might never be known. But it's fair to guess that the surge of emotions caused by music had the same power to bond people as it does today. ***Back in the day, a group that yodeled together probably punched faces less, stayed together for longer, and helped each other more.***

**PSYCH TEST You Come with Preinstalled Software**

Evolution has bestowed humans with amazing, preprogrammed instincts. Some are wonderfully strange, mainly because they are so outdated. Which of the following is one of these curious leftovers?

a. The urge to climb trees.
b. A fascination with sunsets.
c. Scanning open fields for predators.
d. The desire to explore caves.

Some anthropologists believe that the fear of snakes helped humans to evolve **better eyesight**.

## WE STAND TOGETHER TO STAY OFF THE MENU

Humans are pretty defenseless. They have no claws or sharp teeth to fight off a predator—let alone outrun one. So why are humans not the favorite snack of feral dog packs? Researchers believe that your bipedalism (walking on two legs) is a bluff that makes predators think that you are bigger and stronger than you really are. ***Having evolved as a social species that moves in groups also helps, since predators prefer lone pickings.*** Both traits probably came in handy during ancient times when people were more vulnerable to animal attacks.

**PSYCH TEST** **Mythical Creatures with Real Fossils**

When ancient Mediterranean inhabitants found odd skulls, it spawned the belief in one-eyed giants or Cyclopes. But which animal did the fossils belong to?

a. Gorilla.
b. Plesiosaurus.
c. Hippo.
d. Mammoth.

**PSYCH TEST Why We're All Still Huddling Around Fires**

Despite having modern luxuries like heaters and lights, people still love to gather by a fireplace or a bonfire. Explain the evolutionary reason behind this.

a. Fireplace gatherings had a purely social element that still lingers.
b. It allowed people to both socialize and work at night.
c. Fire was the only thing that kept predators at bay.
d. Our ancestors used it for cooking, warmth, and protection.

## GET YOUR TICKETS FOR THE (SHAME) TRAIN

Before getting to the choo choos, let's talk about things with wings. In 1903, when the Wright brothers flew their rickety aircraft into the history books, the public wasn't keen on their claims of success. But that short flight spawned an industry with numerous airlines and gazillions of passengers.

As air travel soared, trains went downhill. The railways became a mode of transportation for those who went on vacation or traveled short distances to work. Even though trains kept a good chunk of travelers, flying is often viewed as a faster and more modern way to get to your destination.

But then climate change stepped onto the stage and a movement began. Called "flight shame," it gained traction when several Swedish celebrities stuck to their promise to swap planes for trains. Many followed in their footsteps, not because they were groupies but because shame really is a factor here. ***Every flight leaves a massive carbon footprint, and this guilts green passengers into abandoning air travel.*** Besides having a smaller carbon impact, trains also offer an emotional perk that more people are craving: to slow down and soak in a scenic route.

**PSYCH TEST Read Receipts Are Anxiety Bombs**

These tick marks show when someone has received and read your phone messages. But when can read receipts become emotionally damaging?

a. People read texts but don't respond.
b. The tick marks disappear due to connectivity issues.
c. They keep showing that messages aren't delivered.
d. Knowing people are tracking your responses with ticks feels invasive.

## THE INCA COMFORTED THEIR SACRIFICIAL VICTIMS

After reading a few books about the Maya and Inca, one might be forgiven for admiring their architects...but recoiling from their love of human sacrifice. The Inca, in particular, had a thing for offering children to the gods. This practice is considered barbaric by most standards today, convincing many that seriously coldhearted individuals ran the show. ***But a recent discovery suggests a softer side to the executioners' mentality.***

Apparently, the adults weren't impervious to the children's fear and sought to comfort them in some cases. But forget about hugs. The Inca way consisted of giving victims alcohol and drugs so they would worry less about their fate. Researchers believed that most of these "cocktails" were designed to excite, but the discovery of three youngsters told a different story.

The Inca had a psychedelic brew called "ayahuasca," and the three young sacrifices, between ages six and seven, had all consumed the concoction. The test results didn't reveal any hallucinogenic compounds in their system, which suggests that the ***inebriating drink was altered to calm the children's anxiety over their upcoming deaths*** and not get them all worked up.

## RAPID ODDITY

**In nineteenth-century England, asylums used music to treat patients, an unusual approach for the time.**

### THE SPOOKS HAUNTING YOUR SMART HOME

Sometimes, the very thing that makes a house appear less haunted—smart technology—seems to be possessed. The lights flicker. Alexa is saying demonic things again. You're not sure whether to ask for a refund or call a priest. So what's going on? ***According to some experts, your psychology can conjure the odd spirit.*** You view devices with certain expectations, and when they glitch or get hacked, this "independent" behavior can pluck a primitive, superstitious nerve that, for a second, makes you wonder whether Beelzebub has possessed the Roomba vacuum.

### PSYCH TEST Phones in the Classroom—Brain Drain or Boost?

Whether they are at high school or university, most students keep their cell phones on them during class. What effect does this have on grades?

a. Phones, as a distraction, can cause grades to fall by 5 percent.
b. Phones, as a research tool, can boost grades by 8 percent.
c. Grades stay the same.
d. Texting during class allows students to work more efficiently on shared projects.

# CHAPTER 2

# DEVELOPMENTAL PSYCHOLOGY: FACTS ABOUT KIDS AND ADULTS

Developmental psychologists follow you from the womb to the tomb—in a noncriminal way, of course! This gaggle of scientists is trying to understand how the mind develops and changes as people age, and more importantly, how it affects behavior during the different stages of life.

This lifelong process is packed to the brim with bizarre mysteries and insights, making it one of psychology's most fascinating branches. Be ready to learn amazing new things about your own age group and other generations in this chapter!

Possessing this knowledge has a deeper purpose than blowing your mind. As a maestro of age-related trivia, you'll understand that many behaviors are developmentally driven, and this could foster a better tolerance for the hiccups between the generations. For example, after reading this chapter, you can tell your mom that there was a legitimate reason why your teenage ears refused to listen when she told you to take out the trash! And no, it wasn't because you were being lazy. Well, maybe not entirely....And decoding the mysterious creature that is the teenager is just the beginning. In the following pages, you'll learn more about babies, young kids, adults, and the elderly. Discover what that kicking baby in the womb is really thinking, why imaginary friends exist for adolescents, and the mystery of the super-ager.

At the end of the day, the scope of developmental psychology is infinitely wide and complex, and it can never be fully covered here. But the trivia in this chapter has been cultivated to give you insights into the different stages of development and to encourage you to learn more about why someone of a particular age, be it a newborn or a centenarian, acts the way they do—and why all of them are equally remarkable!

## THE BRAINY ABILITIES OF BILINGUAL BABIES

One of the most amazing skills babies wow people with is the ability to pick up their mother tongue with effortless grace. But it's their talent for learning two languages simultaneously that might seem like witchcraft to adults who struggle to learn a new language. ***This sorcery boils down to the fact that in infancy, learning happens at a breakneck speed because babies have faster neural formation than their parents.*** While rapidly growing brains explain the genius of baby talkers, scientists have also found that kids from bilingual homes are even more special, developmentally speaking.

This conclusion came from a *Developmental Science* study that entertained eleven-month-olds with English and Spanish conversations while monitoring their brain activity. ***Those who came from English-Spanish homes were actively absorbing both languages without extra stress*** (as an English speaker might experience when attempting to tackle both French and Russian).

But the youngsters from English-only households appeared to have closed the door on new languages. Researchers speculate that after hearing only English for the first six months of their lives, their brains became less sensitive to non-English words, thus making a second language more difficult to learn in the future.

## RAPID ODDITY

Premature babies who listen to music have **better cognitive development** than those who don't.

Until age two, brain growth is **so rapid** that it's considered perhaps the most important developmental life stage.

## BABIES YELL IN THEIR NATIVE LANGUAGE

When a baby starts screaming, most people just hear the noise. A lot of it. But when scientists came together from all over the world and listened to the recorded cries of newborns, they were amazed. ***Even though some of the children were as young as three days old, the wailing mimicked the basics of their mother tongue.*** For instance, the German sprouts cried in a way that lowered their pitch and tone in a downward pattern, or a falling melody contour, while the French babies expressed a rising melody contour. Both are signatures of their respective languages.

### PSYCH TEST That Baby Has Skill!

Infants look pretty much incapable of doing anything except drooling. But which mental skill do babies have before they can even talk?

a. Logical thoughts.
b. Understanding sign language.
c. Grasping parental tone of voice.
d. Highly developed long-term memory.

## PARENTS DEVELOP THEIR OWN LANGUAGE

Most parents develop an unusual dialect when they talk to their baby, aptly called "parentese." Adults all over the world slip into this pattern of speech almost instinctively. The exaggerated speech and sounds should not be confused with baby talk, which is inherently nonsense. ***Parentese relies on real words and grammar.*** Some people believe that children might pick up words faster when they are talked to normally, but the University of Washington found that ***babies are attracted to parentese and that it also boosts their language skills.***

**PSYCH TEST** **Singing the New Dad Blues**

The "fatherhood effect" happens after a child is born. Which negative symptom is associated with this phenomenon?

a. Struggling to sleep.
b. Having little to no motivation.
c. Weight gain.
d. Daydreaming.

## WHY UNBORN BABIES TRAMPLE MOM'S BLADDER

When an unborn baby starts stepping in all the wrong places and makes the mother run for the bathroom, that's accidental. However, the infant is moving for a reason. ***Babies play kick-the-womb to gain awareness and learn more about their surroundings.*** A 2018 study that looked at the brain activity of newborns suggests that acting like the Karate Kid in utero helps babies to create a mental map of the womb. As a bonus, it also provides them with the first awareness of their own bodies.

**PSYCH TEST** **Toddlers Can Recognize Affection Between Adults**

Which sharing habit is recognized by toddlers to signify a special bond between people?

a. Exchanging gifts.
b. Sharing saliva.
c. Wearing similar outfits.
d. Hugging.

## BABIES REALLY ARE OUR OVERLORDS

Wide eyes. Adorable smiles. Gurgling noises. With these magic tricks, babies have their parents at their beck and call. When Oxford scientists looked closer at humanity's overlords, they found that infants are not just designed to appeal to your eyes. Sure, they look cute—and this ensures that parents offer food, clothing, and comfort. ***But their research also revealed that a baby's "Aww" factor appeals to all of your senses***, making said baby far more powerful than you had ever thought possible.

Your caregiver behavior is also awakened by the bubbly laughs, the soft skin, and how babies smell. Such sensory signals travel along a special pathway in the brain and activate neural regions involved in empathy, moral behavior, and play.

But why is it so important for a baby to win hearts? Back in the day, whether in a hunter-gatherer community or a struggling family in Victorian times, raising a child demanded lots of resources. ***Evolution made babies cute to counter the risk of adults abandoning what is, in essence, long years of thankless work***—especially when the child is still too young to fend for themselves.

## RAPID ODDITY

A newborn's **first smile**, when they genuinely beam at someone, happens about six weeks after birth.

**PSYCH TEST** How to Fuel Your Toddler's Meltdown

All parents go through the frustrating phase where their child has a meltdown over the smallest things. Which common emotional response makes the situation worse?

a. The child is scolded or shown other forms of anger.
b. Parents try too hard to be empathetic and calm the child down.
c. The meltdown is ignored.
d. Parents try to distract the child with a toy or snack.

## THE "KIDS THESE DAYS" EFFECT

Every generation grows older, looks over its shoulder, and despairs over all the bad teenagers and young adults these days. Eventually, the latter will also age, sprout a few gray hairs, and do exactly the same thing. According to *Science Advances*, ***five major studies pooled their data and discovered that this illusion is so deeply embedded in humanity that it's almost a knee-jerk reaction***. In other words, even though it happens over and over again, every older generation is convinced that they're the first to get stuck with incapable youths, making them utter, "The kids these days..."

## RAPID ODDITY

Children who are spanked tend to have **lower IQ test scores** than kids who aren't.

## YOUR FIRST LIE IS IMPORTANT!

Perhaps you remember that day well. You stood there with custard on your chin, trying to convince Mom that you did not eat the missing pie. While the consequences that followed your first fib were probably unpleasant, the moment itself was quite significant.

As it turns out, when children begin to lie for the first time, it's not a sign of intentional malice. ***It's a mind shift that takes a child out of the baby brain and into complex mental processes that allow them to understand other people's thoughts.*** Some experts even consider the advent of untruths as a normal milestone for the growing child.

Generally, children tell their first lie around the age of four. Before this age, youngsters just assume that adults know everything. Parents are omnipotent entities who are mind readers, so the idea of deception doesn't dawn on the older toddler until they grasp something life-changing: Parents cannot see through walls, and they cannot read brains. There's a lonely custard pie on the table, and nobody's around...

## TEENAGERS ARE PRIMED TO IGNORE MOM'S VOICE

When researchers played recordings to children of their mother's voices, they discovered a biological sign that Junior was becoming independent. It was so accurate that ***they could tell a kid's age just by looking at the brain's response to Mom's voice***. Kids twelve and younger had explosive activity in the emotional and reward centers of the brain, making them ultra-focused on their parent. But thirteen-year-olds and older showed more reactivity to other people's voices, proving that teens are biologically primed to expand their social circle beyond the home.

## WHY PARENTS ARE CRINGEWORTHY (FOR TWEENS)

When it comes to prickly juveniles, teenagers are not the only age group that slams doors and treats their parents with eye rolls. There's a younger crowd called the "tweens." Roughly aged between nine and twelve, these sprouts are no longer young children—but they also aren't teenagers. Needless to say, they're caught in a weird place.

Experts know that tweens have a complex psychology. They can go from sweet kids who love hugs to sullen youngsters who cringe at everything their parents do. You can emotionally ruin a tween by fluffing their hair in front of their friends. Their life will be over. Yes, melodramatics is another tween trait.

But why do parents catch the brunt of a tween's "rejection"? Even those with a close bond are perplexed at how suddenly Junior squirms away from kisses or clams up about their day. Tweens aren't trying to be hurtful (mostly). ***They're becoming more aware of the world, and social acceptance is hot stuff.*** At this stage, parents just aren't "cool." All is not lost. Psychologists suggest reeling your tween back in with empathy, open talks, and no hair-fluffing.

**PSYCH TEST** **To Redshirt or Not to Redshirt?**

"Redshirting" refers to a parent's decision to delay sending their child to kindergarten. Which negative effect can this have on kids?

a. Children with special needs fall behind.
b. They are bullied for being a year behind.
c. They have delayed social development.
d. They tend to be more lonely at home.

**PSYCH TEST** **Why the Youngest Kid Gets Away with It All**

Households with multiple kids often mete out harsher punishments to the eldest child. What is the reason behind this parenting approach?

a. Parents make an example of the eldest to warn younger siblings.
b. The firstborn is held to higher standards.
c. Older children tend to get into more trouble.
d. Life frustrations make parents turn on the eldest child.

## YOUR FUTURE SELF IS A TOTAL STRANGER

Let's say that you are seventy-six years old. You sit down on a bench next to a fourteen-year-old and discover that it's your teenage self. While such a meeting seems exciting, you're more likely to realize that you are talking to a total stranger.

The longest personality study began in 1947. Over one thousand Scottish teens, aged fourteen, were assessed, and, decades later, 174 agreed to undergo another valuation. The group, whose age averaged seventy-six years, delivered a surprising result: ***Over time, you become a completely different person.***

This was unexpected because personality experiments in the past had suggested that different age groups have stable dispositions. But this was a narrow way to look at the bigger picture. While stability might exist for a few years during your teens, young adulthood, and older years, the Scottish study was the first to consider the entire child-to-elderly spectrum.

But how can there be such a dramatic shift? In most cases, there's nothing dramatic about it. ***Over the years, your behavior undergoes tweaks that are so gradual you often fail to notice whenever you completely shed an old personality.***

## RAPID ODDITY

A *Journal of Environmental Psychology* survey found that kindergarteners think **meat comes from plants** and **French fries come from animals**.

### THE MYSTERY OF THE SUPER-AGERS

Among the elderly, there is a rare group that kind of sounds made up, like something out of the Marvel Universe. In a nutshell, these folks defy the aging process. Unfortunately, nobody is beating *physical* aging just yet, but these super-agers, as they are known, get stuck mentally somewhere in their twenties. Just to clarify, they don't behave like young adults. They act their age, but their recall, reasoning, memory formation, and thinking processes remain so keen that they are on par with people who are roughly in their mid-twenties.

Needless to say, it could be a turning point for humankind to unravel this mystery and use the answers to somehow give everyone a sparkling mind in their old age. Researchers fighting dementia and Alzheimer's disease are particularly happy with the discovery of super-agers. ***Their unusual minds might hold the elusive secret to slowing down degenerative brain disease.*** But unfortunately, for now, it remains unclear why some brains stay youthful.

## RAPID ODDITY

Studies suggest that happiness **peaks** at age eighteen, then again in your mid-sixties.

## RAPID ODDITY

Of all age groups, people in their **forties and fifties** are the best at identifying and understanding emotions in others.

## GRANDAD DEPRESSED? LET HIM ANNIHILATE ALIENS

The statistics for older patients with depression are not the greatest. For instance, only one-third reap any benefits from antidepressants. But a small study from East Carolina University involving eleven well-seasoned citizens offers hope. ***After just four weeks of playing computer games, their symptoms of depression faded.*** Normally, it takes about twelve weeks for elite drugs to achieve the same results. As a bonus, the participants also showed improvement in their thinking, organizing, and planning skills. Puzzle games seem to be the best for elderly depression, but action games can also improve impaired learning and reaction times.

### PSYCH TEST This Perky Emotion Keeps the Brain Sharp

Many physical therapies exist to ease life for the elderly. But which positive feeling can improve cognition in older adults?

a. Feeling in control.
b. Looking forward to something.
c. A loving moment with friends or family.
d. Happiness at achieving a goal.

**PSYCH TEST** **This Is Why Imaginary Companions Sometimes Stay**

When an adolescent has an imaginary friend, is this a positive or negative development, and why?

a. Positive—the teen is creative and social.
b. Positive—it's a fun, harmless way to pass the time.
c. Negative—the child is lonely and socially isolated.
d. Negative—the imaginary friend might be a delusion.

## HOLD MY BEER, I'M FIFTY

When researchers at the University of Oregon studied risk-taking behavior related to age, they only expected to confirm the results of past studies done on the topic. The latter had suggested that a person's competitive streak was strongest during their early twenties, then curved downward after twenty-five. The main reason for this was a decline in hormones, especially those that might be actively promoting high-risk choices, like testosterone and cortisol.

The conventional wisdom of the day was sound. The older you get and the more invested you are in your career, relationships, and pursuits, the more likely it is that taking a big gamble might end in disaster. For example, handing in your notice at the office to impulsively start your own business at home can lead to financial ruin. That's why most people would rather play it safe in their comfort zone, right?

But the Oregon scientists were in for a surprise. The new study included over five hundred men and women of all ages. Instead of turning into couch potatoes after their midlife crisis, ***people's fiery "Hold my beer, I got this," attitude toward a competitive life situation stayed strong until the age of fifty***.

## TAKE THE HAPPY ROAD TO 100 YEARS

As part of the UnitedHealthcare 100@100 yearly survey, interviewers questioned one hundred centenarians. The goal? To understand why some people reach their hundredth birthday. The individuals, all from the US, shared the positive mental tactics they believed helped them to become centenarians. About 60 percent admitted that they were not obsessed with their age and hadn't thought about it for years. Laughing was important to 84 percent of the participants, ***but the most agreed-upon way to stay healthy was to spend time with family—97 percent gave that a thumbs-up***.

**PSYCH TEST** Younger People Have Their Own Midlife Crisis

The midlife crisis is well known. But which feelings underline the quarter-life crisis, which strikes people in their twenties and early thirties?

- **a.** The sense of being trapped, disillusionment, feeling uninspired.
- **b.** Anxiety, frustration, and anger.
- **c.** Depression with a manic edge.
- **d.** Social anxiety, panic disorder, and fear.

## RAPID ODDITY

The adolescent brain's **sensitivity to oxytocin** could explain why teens think everyone's watching them.

## THE MIDDLE AGE FUNK IS GLOBAL

When Dartmouth College and the University of Warwick decided to look at happiness levels, they went all out. To prepare for their study, the institutions gathered information from two million people living in eighty different countries. After crunching the numbers, the researchers noticed ***a global happiness curve that crashed in a person's forties or fifties***. This misery wasn't tied to family life, work, divorce, or income. It mysteriously strikes all genders, singles and couples, the poor and the wealthy. Why this age group is more prone to depression remains a mystery.

## WHY NINE-ENDERS UPEND EVERYTHING

First things first...what the heck is a nine-ender? Well, throughout life, you'll be one of them several times! Nine-enders are people who are about to enter a new decade in their chronological age (in other words, those who turn nineteen, twenty-nine, thirty-nine, etc.).

Since researchers are quick to notice patterns that most of us are not aware of, they detected something interesting about nine-enders. ***When people hit the end of one decade, they make big changes in their lives.*** Sometimes, it's good—they buy a house, chuck a cubicle for a better job, or take the leap and go on a world vacation. But sometimes, it's negative, involving things like extramarital affairs or even suicide.

So what is it that abruptly pushes nine-enders into a positive direction—or down a negative path? According to six studies done in 2015, when people face the end of a decade, they look for existential meaning. This is when feelings of failure can overwhelm someone or prompt them to make a dash for their dreams.

## RAPID ODDITY

**Choir singing** offers the elderly the same cognitive benefits as learning to play a musical instrument.

**PSYCH TEST How the Elderly Brighten Their Own Future**

Growing old is a trying life experience. But which positive psychological factor actually gives some elderly people a better quality of life?

a. Meditating three times a week.
b. Repeating affirmations about self-love.
c. A positive attitude toward aging.
d. Trying new things.

## HOW TO BAKE A COOL KID

Parenting styles are like recipes. Nobody gives you the complete cookbook, so you fill the gaps with a unique blend of your own upbringing experiences, social expectations, and instinct. Sometimes, things go right and kids rise like a champion and go on to be responsible adults. But why do some kids fall flat and key the neighbor's car? While adolescent psychology is complex, the University of New Hampshire discovered that ***parents who raise their kids with respect and not authoritarianism tend to raise respectful, content, and self-reliant offspring***.

## RAPID ODDITY

Babies as young as **eight months old** are aware of, and wary of, aggression in others.

### FEELING YOUNGER THAN YOU ARE? IT'S HEALTHY

The feeling might be frustrating, but it is not uncommon. You feel twenty-eight or thirty, but the person staring back at you from the mirror is forty-five. It's time to swap that frustration for a proud posture. ***Studies from the German Aging Survey have shown that when people feel emotionally younger than their chronological age, they are on the right track to a healthier life.*** They often have more gray matter and physically younger brains. Their risk of mortality is also twice as low as those who feel their age (or older).

**PSYCH TEST** Okay, *Now* I'm Old

Every birthday might add some weight to this feeling, but at what age do most people start to view themselves as getting old?

a. Forty-five.
b. Fifty.
c. Sixty.
d. Seventy.

## RAPID ODDITY

Parents who show anxiety because they're worried about their kids tend to raise **anxious children**.

## TEENS ARE WIRED TO BE OWLS

Across the world, parents struggle with teens who stay up late and refuse to get up in the morning. Research shows that this behavior is normal. ***Teenagers have a different sense of time than the rest of us, and it drives them to be more active at night.*** After the age of twenty, this behavior levels out, and people go to sleep earlier. Modern society isn't doing teenagers any favors. Studies published by the Centers for Disease Control and Prevention indicate that schools start too early for teens (who need to sleep later), causing sleep deprivation, depression, and lower grades.

### RAPID ODDITY

**Juvenoia** is the paranoia that younger generations are flawed and less worthy than older generations.

## EMPTY NESTS MIGHT BE HAPPIER

When children grow up and the last sibling leaves home, young adults might expect their parents to weep and suffer from the famous empty-nest syndrome, which is a form of grief. Researchers found that this is not always the case. In fact, raising kids can put a severe strain on even the healthiest of marriages. Studies published in the journal *Psychological Science* indicate that ***there are many couples whose relationship becomes happier and more satisfying once they wave goodbye to their last sprout***. In such cases, the parents also experience a better sense of well-being and fewer symptoms of depression.

## DO YOU REALLY GET DUMBER AFTER TWENTY?

Past studies "proved" that intelligence peaks in your twenties. But an experiment by MIT shattered this traditional view. As it turns out, intelligence is not a single "thing" that slides downhill after age twenty. It's a multifaceted gem, and ***different areas sparkle the brightest for different age groups***.

The researchers tested 48,537 volunteers between ages ten and eighty-nine. Everyone underwent IQ, memory, and language assessments that scored their working memory, vocabulary, ability to recognize emotions, and aptitude with numbers. That's when the scientists discovered that intelligence peaked in different ways across one's lifetime.

Children and young adults, up to the age of twenty, scored the best on coding tasks involving symbols and numbers. Those in their mid-twenties to mid-thirties aced the working memory tests. Participants in their twenties to the age of forty-eight could accurately name a person's emotions just by looking at photos of eyes. People in their sixties and seventies bested everyone at vocabulary.

The study indicates that people definitely do not grow dumber after twenty. ***Instead, at any given age, people are simultaneously good at some things, getting worse at others, and hitting a plateau with other mental skills.***

**PSYCH TEST** **The Real Age You Become an Adult**

In many countries, people are granted legal adulthood when they turn eighteen. But biologically and psychologically, when are you really all grown up?

- **a.** Twenty.
- **b.** Twenty-five.
- **c.** Twenty-eight.
- **d.** Thirty.

## RAPID ODDITY

Americans who reach the age of seventy are **11 percent more** emotionally stable than people aged twenty-five to thirty-nine.

## A DISEASE CALLED THE "EMPTY HEART"

This condition was first described in 2016 by Chinese professor and mental health professional Xu Kaiwen. He became concerned over the many students who achieved their dream of attending a sought-after university but felt no satisfaction. Instead, they arrived at campus with no sense of purpose and "empty hearts." This is no small matter, either. Many students feel so adrift that they want to end their own lives.

Researchers who looked into the phenomenon found that empty heart disease can happen anywhere in the world, but Chinese youth are particularly at risk. ***Family pressure makes them so single-minded about success that they abandon friendships, hobbies, and sometimes even their real passions and preferred careers.*** Once they "arrive," by stepping into a coveted college or job, almost half of these students view their success as meaningless. This realization, after sacrificing so much, can be devastating.

In the West, many young people do not experience the same intense pressure to be performance superstars. However, they can still experience empty heart disease. Their chronic dread of what the future holds often makes young adults turn to substance abuse.

## RAPID ODDITY

Walking forty minutes a day can **strengthen** the brain structure and power of elderly people.

## THE AMAZING PERKS OF (SORT OF) RAISING YOURSELF

Okay, in no way is anyone suggesting that a toddler should drive themselves to kindergarten! But studies discussed on the *Informed Families* blog indicate that ***young kids who are given more freedom in their own rearing blossom into more confident and resilient young adults than those who are not***. This freedom can take the form of choosing their own outfits and doing their homework without being told to. This can be difficult because modern culture perceives a good parent as someone who regulates every minute of their child's day. However, this can teach kids learned helplessness (the belief that there is nothing they can do to change their lot) that might remain with them beyond childhood.

### PSYCH TEST Teenage Love Burns Brightly and Fast

Teenagers are notorious for their heated romances—but also for relationships that flame out after a few weeks. Why is this?

a. Most relationships are easy flings.
b. The passion is there but not the emotional commitment.
c. Teen couples argue more than adults.
d. Their heavy load at school and home gets in the way.

## RAPID ODDITY

Karate training **lowers depression** in seniors and gives them better self-esteem.

**PSYCH TEST** **Okay, Maybe You're Not Grounded!**

Grounding is a popular way to discipline rule-breaking kids. But which negative psychological consequence of grounding actually makes the parent-child bond worse?

a. Grounding never works; it causes more conflict.
b. Both parties are more prone to depression.
c. It removes a child's personal power, leading to resentment.
d. Grounding is an excuse to not talk things out.

## OVER EIGHTEEN? JOIN THE FAN CLUB

Thanks to ageism, most cultures believe that being a fan is only acceptable when you're a child or a teenager. Everyone else is expected to grow up and bury the "unimportant" things that they were once passionate about. But according to psychologists, those who remain a lifelong fan of a particular sports team, band, hobby (or anything else, really) can look forward to a powerful benefit. ***Being a follower can give people anchors—something that stays stable when everything else changes.*** Anchors can provide resilience in hard times, especially as fans grow older.

## RAPID ODDITY

Research from a University College London neuroscientist suggests that fourteen-year-olds show the **riskiest behavior** of all teens.

## CASUAL FRIENDSHIP IS A LONGEVITY POTION

In a study published in *Psychology and Aging*, scientists trooped after a group of volunteers for thirty years. When the participants hit middle age, their friendships revealed why twenty-somethings are so social and why their knack for casual buddies is not as pointless as it seems.

To explain why this is significant, let's back it up a little. Science has already proven that high-quality friendships are beneficial for your mental and physical health. Indeed, older people with no social connections face the same early mortality rate as smokers.

***The key to keeping a few bosom buds is to learn to be a good friend yourself, especially when it comes to accepting people for who they are.*** This is how casual friendships can lay the foundation for the real thing. According to the study, your twenties introduce you, often for the first time, to friends with different values, backgrounds, and personalities. This is when you learn to play nice, despite your differences!

***Those who do so successfully can look forward to several perks that come with long-term bonds***, including a longer life, a sense of belonging, reduced stress, and social support when the road gets bumpy.

### PSYCH TEST Loneliness Pounces Thrice

Scientists have discovered that loneliness peaks at three ages/age groups. Pick the unlucky trio.

a. The late twenties, mid-fifties, and late eighties.
b. Age eighteen, forty-five, and eighty.
c. The early thirties, mid-forties, and late eighties.
d. Age sixteen, the late twenties, and early sixties.

## RAPID ODDITY

Older adults with pets visit the doctor less often and **enjoy better life satisfaction**.

**PSYCH TEST** **Home Is Where These Benefits Are**

Growing older at home, not in a nursing facility, comes with amazing physical and mental health benefits. Choose the top perks of aging in place.

a. Less stress and fewer problems.
b. Sharper cognition and increased energy levels.
c. Better relationships, positivity, and less pain.
d. More tranquility and greater health.

### THE BRIGHT SIDE OF CHORES (FOR KIDS, NOT YOU!)

It's an age-old question: Should you make your kids do chores? If you're a pro-chores parent, you can look forward to doing fewer tasks yourself! But what benefits do the kids get? When researchers asked this question, they looked at sprouts of different ages and found something interesting. Kindergarten kids with chores, even small tasks, ***enjoy a remarkable array of perks***. It teaches them to interact amicably with family and how to make choices. Years later, the same kids also showed better social skills, life satisfaction, and academic skills.

## RAPID ODDITY

Making friends is **easier** in childhood because you trust and invest more easily in others.

Giving toddlers **fewer toys** can improve their focus and their ability to play more creatively.

## TODDLERS—THE CUPS THAT OVERFLOW

Well, that's one way to describe a tantrum! But that's essentially what happens when a toddler has a meltdown. According to scientists, tantrums aren't a sign that young children are being difficult on purpose. ***It's the only way toddlers can have some release when a surge of strong emotions overwhelms them.*** Parents might feel alone when their kid blows up in a crowded restaurant, but they're actually not. According to a study published by the National Library of Medicine, a whopping 91 percent of children, aged thirty to thirty-six months, have a daily meltdown. Roughly 87 percent of eighteen- to twenty-four-month-olds also hug the floor and scream.

**PSYCH TEST** Kids Lie to Parents Who Lie about Santa

Most kids figure out by themselves that Santa Claus isn't real. Why do some pretend to their parents that they still believe?

a. To keep the spirit of Christmas alive.
b. They want presents.
c. Kids like fooling their parents.
d. They view it as a family game.

## RAPID ODDITY

Many adults still sleep with a **security blanket** or a **plush toy** from their childhood.

## ROSE-TINTED GLASSES COME IN KID SIZES

Tantrums aside, young children are natural optimists. Grownups only relax their guard around new situations or people when things go well for a while. But kids are less cautious. ***According to researchers, most youngsters have a rosy view of the world, and this positivity bias makes them see the best in others, themselves, and animals.***

A 2013 study looked at children aged three through seven. This crowd can be easily swayed by positive statements and behavior, even when it comes from a total stranger. For example, the six- and seven-year-olds trusted a zookeeper who told them good things about unfamiliar animals. During another test, some preschoolers were told that their peers had drawn better pictures than they did, but the tots stayed positive and believed that their own artwork still rocked.

A plausible reason for this bias could be learning. This age group is at a critical juncture of physical and cognitive development. ***Being optimistic about everything could be nature's way of encouraging children to keep exploring and learning as much as they can about the world around them.***

## PREDICTABLE PARENTING IS BRAIN FOOD FOR KIDS

Childhood has a huge impact on how you behave and think as an adult. Since parents play a major role in what their kids see, hear, and experience, a University of California study decided to search for a link between parental behavior and the development of their offspring's brain. After fifteen years of experiments, the researchers discovered that ***when kids view their parents as predictable, their brain circuits—especially the emotional connections—were healthier than those of their peers who faced inconsistent parenting***. The latter group might also be at a higher risk of mental illness or substance abuse.

**PSYCH TEST** The Summer Brain Drain

The "summer slide" describes how students tend to forget what they've learned in school while on vacation. Why does this happen?

a. The brain removes new, unused information.
b. Children deliberately bury their "boring" lessons to enjoy summer.
c. Students never properly absorbed the information in the first place.
d. Only kids with neural problems experience the slide.

### RAPID ODDITY

Housebound elderly people become very **attached to windows** because they're a connection to the outside world.

## TODDLERS DON'T GET HIDE-AND-SEEK

Young kids love to play this popular game. Some parents also find it amusing because their toddlers "hide" in strange ways. Indeed, some youngsters just cover their eyes while hiding in full view. But why are preschoolers so terrible at hide-and-seek, even when the rules are explained to them?

In the past, psychologists thought that toddlers are so egocentric that they believe everyone thinks—and, more importantly, sees—like them. So, by covering their own eyes, nobody can see them. But studies from 2012 proved otherwise. When toddlers were shown an adult who covered her eyes, the kids insisted that she was invisible. When she covered her mouth, they claimed they couldn't hear her speak.

This sounds weird, but it could explain the real reason why preschoolers close their eyes when they hide. They believe in a two-way connection. ***In other words, the seeker must make eye contact with the players who are hiding in order to uncloak their "invisibility."*** This is why toddlers cannot be entirely egocentric. Instead, they appear to be very aware that people are in constant interaction with each other.

## HOW TO SPOT A BUDDING INTROVERT

Toddlers are famous for their nonstop talking. It can grate on one's nerves, for sure, but parents with unusually bashful and quiet toddlers worry that their child might have developmental issues—more specifically, a cognitive problem, a language delay, or both. But recent studies have shown that some toddlers who keep quiet when spoken to understand everything that is being said to them. They just choose not to respond. ***Indeed, in most cases, there is nothing wrong with them; they are just the introverts of the future!***

## TODDLERS DON'T APPRECIATE WHINERS

The Max Planck Institute gathered forty-eight toddlers to see how this emotionally charged group would react to tantrums in others. The three-year-olds interacted with adults who acted out several scenarios. The kids thought these were genuine displays of negative emotions, and the results were interesting!

In one experiment, a man reacted to something that caused him "genuine" distress (the lid of a toy box slammed shut on his hand). In another display, an adult overreacted when his sleeve got caught on the lid. The latter scenario was designed to show the kids an example of someone going ape over something unimportant.

The kids showed concern for the adults when they were justifiably upset or when their distress had an unknown cause. ***This proved not only that three-year-olds can assess people's anguish levels but also that they had less sympathy for the crybabies.*** In a final experiment, toddlers were given two balloons. An adult then "lost" his only balloon and became upset. The kids were more likely to give one of their balloons to the man if they'd seen him become agitated for a good reason in the previous experiments.

**PSYCH TEST Another Secret Ingredient to Hit 100**

Genetics plays a role, but which social and psychological factors can also help you reach that big, one-hundredth birthday bash?

- **a.** The ability to live independently while staying with family.
- **b.** Having a happy network of friends.
- **c.** Mixed-age communities and a pro-aging environment.
- **d.** Class exercise and therapy.

**PSYCH TEST** **Why Toddlers Pooh-Pooh Your Commands**

A lot of orders given to preschoolers seem to fall on deaf ears. Pick the correct toddler mindset that explains this.

a. They're being difficult on purpose.
b. Toddlers cannot prepare for the future.
c. They don't understand the order.
d. Toddlers are easily distracted and then forget their instructions.

## WHEN SIBLINGS LOSE TO PETS

Some kids prefer to bond with a pet rather than their sibling. When researchers wanted to take a closer look at this preference, the goal was to understand the psychological reasons why siblings don't make the cut. The UK researchers interviewed seventy-seven kids, all aged twelve, and discovered that dogs were the favorite furry pal to claim this honor. ***The youngsters admitted that they talked to their pets and even confided secrets in them.*** Although the study failed to determine a definite reason for this preference, one possible explanation could be that dogs, unlike some siblings, are nonjudgmental.

## RAPID ODDITY

Enjoying games as adults is regarded by society as unimportant, but playing promotes **relaxation, empathy, social skills, and creativity**.

CHAPTER 3

# BIOPSYCHOLOGY AND BEHAVIORAL PSYCHOLOGY:

## THE BIOLOGY AND BIASES THAT INFLUENCE YOUR BEHAVIOR

Why do humans behave the way they do? This question is older than the first communal cave, and we still scratch our heads in wonder and confusion over what other people do and why—and sometimes, in dismay at our own conduct. (*Did I seriously just buy a dancing beer can for fifty bucks? It seemed like a great idea at the time...*) Sound familiar? Maybe you don't make any impulse buys. But what about all those times when you couldn't quite explain why you behaved in a certain way? Sometimes, the brain just seems to have a mind of its own...

Hold that thought. Psychologists understand that there is a deep connection between the brain and behavior. At first blush, that seems rather obvious! However, many of your thoughts are triggered by cognitive biases and brain chemicals that secretly nudge you to act in certain ways—mostly without your awareness.

As you become more aware of the things that pull your strings from the shadows, you can live more deliberately. How? By diving into two amazing branches of psychology! Biopsychology looks at how the biology of the brain influences behavior, while behavioral psychology studies how the mind can do the same.

Both fields are packed with explanations about human behavior, and this chapter is filled with trivia from these strange corners of your wonderful brain. Discover the reason why you feel drawn to the edge when in a high place, why you bought that dancing beer can, and when and why you sleep like a dolphin!

## THE BREAKFAST LOOP

Food is a great source of pleasure, especially when a variety of tasty treats are on the table. But when scientists looked at the morning habits of people living in the US and France, they discovered something peculiar. On most days, the hungry test subjects did not seek out variety. Instead, they prepared the same breakfast every morning. Even when boredom with the food set in, people still reached for the same toast or cereal brand.

***As it turns out, those who stick to one breakfast tend to assign mealtimes with a specific purpose or need.*** While lunch and dinner represent flavor, favorites, and even fancy restaurants, breakfast is a workhorse with two jobs. After a long night of sleep, most people don't have the time or energy to whip up a new, complex breakfast each morning. For this reason, tucking into eggs every day combats busy mornings and groggy minds by providing a quick, high-calorie meal.

**PSYCH TEST** **Food Experts Hate This Ancient Craving**

Which dietary craving is the bane of nutritionists but also a hardwired human instinct?

a. Red meat.
b. Salt.
c. Fatty foods.
d. Sugar.

## RAPID ODDITY

Falling in love is **biochemically identical** to having obsessive-compulsive disorder.

## THERE'S A REASON YOU CAN'T LET GO OF BIG MISTAKES

Sometimes, a mistake is obvious to everyone except the person who is bubbling underwater with the ship. That new business you worked so hard to put together is now consuming more funds than creating profit. Or what about those expensive (and yet super-uncomfortable) high heels you wear because you just *have* to get your money's worth even if it means growing a wayward toe? ***This refusal to give up on something that you've invested a lot in, even though it's doing more harm than good, is known as "sunk cost bias."***

## THE VOID IS CALLING

The French call it *l'appel du vide*: "the call of the void." ***This term refers to the impulse to suddenly jump off a dangerously high bridge or building.*** You might be hiking with friends or thinking about trail mix snacks when you see a ledge nearby. Out of the blue, you just get this thought: "What if I stepped off this cliff right now?" And not like an accident either. On purpose.

Researchers studying the phenomenon haven't found any links between this concerning behavior and the desire for self-harm. Instead, the thought occurs spontaneously among healthy-minded individuals, and the urge to act on the impulse passes quickly. Most people who experience it feel a little shocked because it's so out of character for them. The good news is that few people listen to the call, which is also known as the "high place phenomenon."

Evidence suggests that a brain glitch might be behind the mystery. When sensing danger, the mind tells you to move away from the ledge. ***But instead of being pushed back by fear, imagination takes things too far and triggers the scary thought of "What if...?"***

## SOMETIMES, YOU SLEEP LIKE A DOLPHIN

When dolphins snooze, half of their brain stays alert. If a great white shark creeps closer, those sleeping dolphins will know it. Humans do the same thing. All right, you don't sleep in the ocean, and you certainly don't have to worry about sharks at night, yet something amazing happens when you sleep in a new location.

The safety-loving brain is not comfortable with unfamiliar bedrooms because it doesn't know if there is a saber-toothed cat hiding in the laundry basket. And since you are most vulnerable when you sleep, the body then primes itself to stay alert for danger.

***During the "first night effect," the right side of the brain drools into the pillow while the left side goes into full bodyguard mode.*** The phenomenon could be the reason why you feel so bushed after sleeping in a new place. Half of your brain is sleep-deprived! Interestingly, a second night in the same place will not provoke the same response. Should the first night pass uneventfully, then your whole brain will sleep on the second night. This is also why sleep researchers often discard the first night's data in experiments.

### PSYCH TEST A Popular Magic Trick Exposed

A popular trick is to take a normal pencil and wiggle it up and down. Why does it suddenly appear to be made of soft rubber?

a. The brain and eyes can't keep up with the movement.
b. It's a trick of the light.
c. Sleight of hand.
d. It's a trick pencil.

## THIS GROUP HAS ZERO RACIAL BIAS

Nowhere in the world, in any culture, is there a human population without racial stereotypes. Studies from the American Psychological Association have shown that children as young as three prefer their own ethnic group. Except for kids born with Williams syndrome. ***This genetic disorder makes kids super-friendly with all races.*** They even lack the normal jitters that most people would feel when talking to a group of strangers. The rare condition is ironic, though, as it doesn't foster complete equality. Despite their openness with everyone, kids with Williams syndrome still cling to gender stereotypes.

### RAPID ODDITY

The "**halo effect**" is a bias that suggests attractive people are more intelligent than others.

## THE REAL LIVING DEAD (THEY'RE ALIVE)

The mind can play cruel tricks. But nothing compares to the bizarre reality of those with Cotard's delusion. ***This syndrome can convince a person that everything they see doesn't exist.*** The situation deepens when they turn their focus on themselves and believe that they're either missing a limb or that they've died. No evidence to the contrary can convince a sufferer that both their legs are still there or that they are not deceased. Thankfully, the syndrome is very rare, with only about two hundred cases on record.

## YOUR WALLET OVERSPENDS, NOT YOU!

Overspending can happen seemingly on its own. Blame a cognitive bias called the "leverage bias." ***This sneaky goober tricks you into thinking that you are wealthier than you really are.*** Amazingly, this perception doesn't change for some people even when the cost of living goes up and their net worth remains the same. This skewed perception isn't rare, either. When a university in Milan tested a group of volunteers by giving them pots of digital money to manage, about 78 percent failed to correctly perceive their own financial worth.

**PSYCH TEST** There's Always Room for Sugar

Which neural reward system makes people okay with eating sugar on a daily basis but not the same cooked meal every day?

a. A physical energy boost.
b. Higher oxytocin levels.
c. A spike in dopamine.
d. Better mental focus.

## DID THAT KISS LACK MAGIC? BLAME YOUR HAND

Thought your smooching technique was spontaneous and all you? Well, not entirely. The brain manages a legion of tasks by controlling them with either the left or right hemisphere, and researchers have discovered that kissing is closely connected to one's dominant hand. ***Right-handed individuals prefer to zoom in on their partner from the right, while left-handed people tend to tilt their heads to the left.*** This response is so hardwired that when you canoodle from the opposite direction you normally would, the kiss actually feels wrong.

## FOUND WHAT YOU'RE LOOKING FOR? BEWARE THE SATISFACTION!

There is a little-known cognitive bias called "satisfaction of search," or SOS. This mental hiccup is no small matter. It can lead to serious mistakes, especially in the fields of security and medicine.

Satisfaction of search is that satisfying feeling you get when you find something you've been looking for. ***But for some reason, the brain then becomes primed to look for similar items and overlook equally important but unrelated things.*** For example, when airport security discovers that you're smuggling a questionable sandwich into the country, they look for more snacks. The chances that they will find that saltshaker you pilfered from a Tibetan temple then drop dramatically.

***The problem is so serious that some countries now follow the advice of SOS researchers and isolate airport staff who search bags for contraband.*** By allowing them to work without distractions, their mental focus improves and so does their ability to find second and third types of illegal goods. To save lives, doctors are also trained to ignore the satisfaction of finding a bone fracture on an X-ray and to continue searching for unrelated signs of disease.

**PSYCH TEST** This Is Why You Struggle to Pick a Pizza

Imagine you're looking at a menu. You see several amazing meals. But why is it so hard to pick the item that you want?

**a.** Too many choices incapacitate the brain.
**b.** You feel anxious about eating in public.
**c.** The pressure to choose is too much.
**d.** You cannot focus with all the noisy patrons.

## IMPOSTERS MAKE GREAT EMPLOYEES

Those with imposter syndrome fear that their skills suck, and it's only a matter of time before others realize this too. But look at that wall honoring the Employee of the Month, and you'll find a couple of imposters there. ***Indeed, the deep-seated need to avoid being "caught" makes them put their best foot forward at the office.*** Several studies involving over 3,600 employees showed that these self-doubters are team players with good social skills, two traits that even the grumpiest boss would appreciate.

### RAPID ODDITY

The **false consensus effect** makes people overestimate how much others agree with their own worldview.

## THE NEAR-DEATH REEL MIGHT BE REAL

Countless near-death reports detail how victims often witness their life flash before their eyes. But despite all the testimonies, there was no solid evidence of the phenomenon's existence. It took an unfortunate event to provide scientists with proof. In 2016, a man passed away during a brain scan. The images showed that for one minute (thirty seconds before his death and thirty seconds afterward), ***his brain waves resembled those seen in dreaming, memory, and recall—the perfect combination to have your life flash before your eyes.***

## RAPID ODDITY

Pleasure-wise, the brain makes **no distinction** between lovemaking and listening to great music.

### THE BRAIN IS A TROUBLE MAGNET

Have you ever wondered why your life sometimes feels like a tornado of never-ending problems? The experience might not be entirely accurate. True problems aside, the majority of things that irritate or bother you on a daily basis are not a direct threat. They're small annoyances, and most tend to evaporate on their own.

But even when your life is going very well, your brain will poke you with a stick and say, "Hey, let's worry about that thing that's never bothered you before." In psychology, this is termed "moving the goalposts." ***In other words, the goal keeps changing for your brain—and it usually happens the moment it solves a problem.*** Looking to solve the next problem and finding none, your brain then turns on people and situations it had previously dismissed as harmless and views them in a less favorable light. Presto. New problems.

While this is a genuine misfire for the brain, it feels very real to you. So the next time you worry too much about nothing in particular, just know that your mind probably pulled up those posts and moved them again!

## RAPID ODDITY

Financial biases can make people **underestimate** the cost of a loan, leading to heavy debts.

## HOW HIGH STAKES SQUASH YOUR DREAMS

Most people dream of doing something wonderful. Maybe it's getting the corner office at work, the one that comes with prestige and stunning benefits. Perhaps you are on the cusp of qualifying for the Olympics after dedicating years of your life to a particular sport. But between the realms of hoping and holding the prize lies a No Man's Land where people go to choke.

***Sure enough, there is something about high stakes that leads to poor performance.*** Caltech's researchers wanted to find out why, so they roped in a couple of volunteers. The participants who successfully completed a challenging test could win nothing or a cash amount of up to $100. Those with the least incentive generally performed better, while the volunteers who stood to win the most failed more often.

Other studies support this outcome. ***The more apprehensive a person feels about losing a prize, promotion, or similar future benefits, the more likely they are to worry about failure.*** The stress over this perceived loss tends to snowball and negatively affect performance.

### PSYCH TEST Give Your Biases the Boot—and Win This Prize!

Which beneficial results can you expect when you work to overcome your own biases?

- **a.** The ability to see others' biased behaviors.
- **b.** Recognizing people and situations for who and what they really are.
- **c.** A noticeable reduction in stress.
- **d.** The ability to hide your biases from other people.

## READING THIS BOOK IS GOOD FOR YOUR HEALTH

Ah, trivia. Ever wonder why you love it? According to psychologists, learning novel facts is similar to gambling. ***Just like winning a bet, you get a surge of dopamine whenever trivia proves to be thrilling, like when you learn something fascinating or score a correct answer.*** But unlike gambling, there are no negative consequences. Those who love trivia nights at the local pub can also look forward to benefits like socializing and better self-esteem. Bonus: If you excel at trivia, researchers believe that your brain is wired more efficiently than most!

**PSYCH TEST** The Bias That Separates Us

Confirmation bias is something that everyone has. What is the main trademark of this self-serving and powerful instinct?

a. Putting subtle pressure on others to conform to your beliefs.
b. Cherry-picking friends and information to support your own beliefs.
c. Always assuming the worst, to prepare for the worst.
d. An increase in deceptive behavior when you feel threatened.

## YOU'RE BEING FRAMED—AT THE GROCERY STORE

Aptly called the "framing effect," this cognitive bias can lead you down the wrong path when making decisions. It appears when a person is given a limited number of choices, and the wording rather than pertinent information influences their final decision. ***It's particularly powerful when the words are framed positively—even when the negative version says exactly the same thing.*** For example, you're more likely to grab the cleaner that claims to murder 99 percent of germs than an identical product that says, "We let 1 percent of all germs live."

## RAPID ODDITY

The desire to spend time outdoors is **strongly influenced** by your genetic makeup.

### THE INVISIBLE GORILLA EXPERIMENT

In 1999, researchers asked volunteers to watch a video of people throwing a ball to their teammates. One team wore white shirts and the other team wore black. The volunteers had to count how many times the white team passed the ball.

Nobody was told that a person in a gorilla suit was going to appear between the two teams—but appear he did. A short while into the video, the gorilla walked in, stood at the center of the moving groups, and beat his chest. Then, he ambled out of sight.

Remarkably, when the clip ended and the volunteers were asked if they had noticed anything unusual, roughly half of them said no. They completely missed the gorilla, despite its hairiness and chest-thumping. ***Psychologists call such bloopers "inattentional blindness."***

This cognitive bias is funny when someone tells you a gorilla stood right in front of you. But this blindness, which is caused by a lack of attention, can lead to serious road accidents when you fail to notice a car trying to speed by and push in front of you.

## RAPID ODDITY

Procrastinators have **enlarged fear centers** (the amygdala), meaning that risk aversion, not laziness, holds them back.

**Cognitive biases** are subconscious errors the brain makes while trying to simplify a complex world.

## THIS HOBBY MYSTIFIES PSYCHOLOGISTS

Some collections appear so mundane that observers just shake their heads. But collectors don't care. They will passionately add another bottle cap or shell to their collection. ***When neurologists looked into this behavior, they realized that there's no one answer to explain people's love affair with collecting.*** Some reasons could include a link to the past, nursing a unique cache, and even the satisfaction of organizing the items. Novelty also plays a role. This feeling activates the brain's pleasure center, which might explain why collectors feel the urge to keep finding and examining their next "prize."

**PSYCH TEST** The Bias That Foils Your Yearly Resolutions

Making New Year's resolutions can provoke excitement and dedication to see major goals through. Why do 90 percent of people abandon their plans within weeks?

a. They underestimate how much effort it takes to achieve big goals.
b. People change their New Year's plans a lot.
c. These plans were never serious.
d. Life gets in the way.

## RAPID ODDITY

**"Zombie behaviors"** are subconscious but complex actions, like typing, standing, or quickly estimating a distance.

### THE BENEFITS OF SNARK

You've just won the Employee of the Month Award. The office bully shakes his head and says, "Aren't *you* special?" If you recognize that he's being hurtful—and not congratulatory—then well done! You have what neurologists would view as a normal, healthy brain. And so does the bully. Indeed, the inability to dispense or notice sarcasm might be a sign of brain disease. ***Other benefits of being a sarcastic person (or snark detector) include creative problem-solving skills and sharper memory.***

**PSYCH TEST** When Randomness Looks Meaningful

Your mind is searching for patterns—even where there are none. Which cognitive bias causes people specifically to see a pattern in random events?

a. The clustering illusion.
b. The pattern bias.
c. Pareidolia.
d. The sequence bias.

**PSYCH TEST The Brain's Vanishing Act**

The Troxler effect describes the brain's ability to make something disappear in front of your eyes. What is the psychological benefit of this?

a. By deleting unimportant information, you can focus on what matters.
b. It prevents the formation of useless memories.
c. It helps you to not become overwhelmed by lots of visual information.
d. It soothes the nervous system.

## AIM FOR BRONZE INSTEAD OF SILVER!

As a fan of psychology, you don't need to be told that humans often behave in unexplained ways! But one quirk surprised even the experts. When psychologists combed through photos of Olympic medal ceremonies, they consistently noticed sad faces on the podium. Contrary to what one might think, these were not the bronze medalists. In fact, those who came in third beamed with extreme happiness. ***No, the sad-looking competitors were the silver medal winners.***

This unusual behavior stems from how competitors view their situations. Bronze medalists think about the person who placed fourth and just missed the podium. This makes bronze winners thank their stars that they've made it onto an Olympic podium. Silver medalists look up at the person who came in first place. They're plagued with unhelpful thoughts about what they could've done better. Some silver medalists are crushed because they were a fraction of a second slower than the winner.

So if you have Olympic aspirations and want to have a grand time on the podium, aim for first or third place!

## SOME PEOPLE LOSE THEIR SHEEP

Can't sleep? Try counting sheep! This age-old snooze hack is all about boring yourself to sleep by visualizing and counting animals as they merrily jump over a fence. People with aphantasia can never do this. ***The brain condition is basically a blind mind's eye.*** Sufferers cannot summon images of their family or anything else, really. When they do try, what they "see" is normally just a black space. Deepening the mystery is the fact that this condition doesn't seem to affect their artistic creativity and imagination.

## THIS IMMUNE SYSTEM RUINS YOUR DATES

Did you know that you have two amazing immune systems? The first is the physiological immune system that fights infections. The second is what psychologists refer to as the "behavioral immune system." Unlike the first immune system, it has a powerful say over your mind and decisions. ***Curiously, it appears to weed out unsuitable romantic partners!***

According to scientists, your second immune system's purpose is much the same as the other system's: It's trying to protect you from diseases. The main way to activate the behavioral immune system is with the mind itself—a fact the researchers discovered when they grossed out volunteers by telling them disgusting hygiene facts before sending them on a speed-dating circuit.

The volunteers who were wary of germs were more standoffish in the dating room than those who didn't mind the odd bug. The reason behind the backpedaling might explain why you sometimes impulsively ax a date! Once the brain detects the subconscious signals of unease, it activates an immune response, getting all your white blood cells ready to fight. ***It also shuts down romantic zeal to prevent physical contact and possible contamination.***

## RAPID ODDITY

The **blind spot bias** makes you think you don't have any biases—when you do!

## A MYSTERIOUS BIAS HIDES YOUR PAIN FROM DOCTORS

Many biases hamper the medical world, but one is particularly *ouch*. A study published in the *Proceedings of the National Academy of Sciences* found that ***doctors are less likely to dispense painkillers at the end of a long night shift***. The drivers behind this bias aren't clear, but researchers suggest that tiredness can lower a doctor's empathy levels for patients and impair their ability to correctly assess someone's pain. This isn't proof that all doctors have a bad attitude at the end of their shifts! The study found that medical experts who only want the best for their patients are also susceptible to this bias.

**PSYCH TEST** Speaking with Spooks

For centuries, spiritualists have claimed to hear the voices of the dead. Which condition could be fueling this belief?

a. Schizophrenia.
b. Auditory hallucinations.
c. Delusions.
d. Pathological lying.

## RAPID ODDITY

People with **similar body odor** often click as friends during their first meeting.

## RAPID ODDITY

Your brain **loves spring-cleaning** because it brings a sense of peace and accomplishment.

## WHY EVERYONE'S STARING AT YOU

Well...unless you're making a public scene, they might not *actually* be looking at you! ***We all have this bias, called the "spotlight effect," that makes us overestimate just how much other people are staring at us.*** Research has shown that neither positive nor negative events, like scoring a goal or spilling coffee on yourself at a café, provoke as much attention from others as you believe. This is good news for those who have social anxiety (but not so much for those who like the limelight)!

**PSYCH TEST** Uncontrollable Nighttime Munchies

Most eating happens consciously—and during the day. Which biological hiccup causes people to get up and eat while still asleep?

a. Narcolepsy.
b. Desynchronized circadian rhythm.
c. A nocturnal spike in stress hormones.
d. Abnormal craving impulses.

## RAPID ODDITY

Preparing a meal can **desensitize** your appetite. That's why food prepared by others tastes better.

## RAPID ODDITY

Introverts are **more stimuli-sensitive**. When tasting lemons, introverts produce 50 percent more saliva than extroverts.

### DYSLEXIA'S AMAZING TRUE PURPOSE

For a long time, dyslexia was viewed as a learning disorder and nothing more. Experts only focused on how those with dyslexia tend to fall behind with their education or struggle to navigate a world that runs on the written word. But a recent study discovered that the neurological condition has benefits.

Researchers were curious about the fact that dyslexia is both common and strongly influenced by inheritable genes. This suggested to them that, in the distant past, evolution favored dyslexia for some reason. ***They also pondered on past studies that showed how people with dyslexia tend to be more inventive, and they often also predict the outcome of situations better than others.***

In prehistoric times, this would've given people with dyslexia a survival edge. In an unpredictable, dangerous world, being able to predict outcomes correctly and to creatively solve problems often meant the difference between life and death.

Evolution never intended for dyslexia to cause reading difficulties. Humans hadn't had writing or reading skills for thousands of years before literacy became a thing. Before then, people with dyslexia wouldn't even have realized that something was different about their brains.

## THE REAL REASON WHY PENALTY KICKS TURN SOUR

Soccer fans cannot understand the following scenario. Their team is so awesome that they made it to the final of an international championship. The game's outcome depends on a penalty kick, and then the top kicker flakes. They suddenly have two left feet and appear to have forgotten all their training.

When it comes to a high-pressure goal, it doesn't matter if the player has a million awards for stupendous ability on the soccer field. ***If they cannot control their negative thoughts, their performance will choke on the spot.*** That's easier said than done. Being chosen as your team's representative for a penalty shoot-out in international soccer puts you in one of the most pressured situations in the sporting world.

Even the best players, like David Beckham, have reported not being able to think normally—or even breathe normally—right before trotting up to the ball for a penalty kick. ***Research also shows that this anxiety can constrict muscles and increase heart rate.*** Sometimes, especially when coupled with mental stress, these symptoms can lead to the infamously bad kicks that make fans groan.

## WANT TO RUIN SUNDAY? JUST THINK ABOUT MONDAY!

Your thoughts drive many of your behaviors, but there is probably nothing as universally experienced as the "Sunday scaries." ***This is when you begin to feel anxious and overwhelmed on a Sunday, usually in the afternoon or evening.*** The reason? Because the next day is a whole new week filled with responsible adulting. According to psychologists, people have different degrees of the scaries. Most people develop anxious thoughts, an upset stomach, headaches, and insomnia. However, in extreme cases, the stress can be so severe that some people suffer a heart attack.

## HOW TO MAKE YOURSELF SICK WITH RELAXATION

For this tutorial, you need to start with a good dose of stressful activities, the longer the better. Perhaps a demanding work project or maybe a personal problem that takes weeks of effort and adrenaline to solve! Super, now you are set for the next step. Step two? Relax. And before you know it, you have a mysterious reaction that includes severe fatigue, stuffy sinuses, and perhaps even something resembling a bad case of the flu.

This is known as the "let-down effect," and it certainly lets down a lot of people. After going through a tough time, it's only natural to look forward to a well-earned rest or vacation. However, it's not uncommon to get sick instead and spend your days clutching a tissue instead of a martini. So what gives?

***During prolonged periods of stress, your body runs on a cocktail of stress hormones and adrenaline.*** This keeps the immune system in peak condition because the brain thinks you're in some kind of danger. When the situation resolves and you relax, the chemicals disappear and the immune system becomes suppressed, turning you into a sitting duck for the next virus that floats your way.

**PSYCH TEST** **The Mistakes That Mortify You Are Cute**

Most people fear looking foolish in front of others. But why do bystanders often view your fumbling moments in a positive light?

a. Not being perfect makes you endearing.
b. It's harmless humor to see someone a little embarrassed.
c. The incident lightens the mood for everybody.
d. It's the polite thing to do.

## YOU DON'T NEED WORDS TO THINK

For many years, well-respected experts suggested that you can't think without words. At least not complicated, intelligent thoughts. In recent times, psychologists had a gut feeling that this widely accepted view wasn't true.

There were already grounds for believing that language isn't necessary for reasoning. Decades of studies proved that not everyone has an inner monologue, or discussion, with themselves when they think—and these people are not dunces. They are healthy, functioning adults. Even so, the scientific community clung to the idea that words are a critical ingredient for complex thoughts.

To test this, an MIT researcher named Evelina Fedorenko asked volunteers to silently solve Sudoku games or algebra problems. While the participants worked, brain scans watched their every move. If words were essential to higher reasoning, then the scans would detect activity in the brain areas for language as well as logic. ***However, as the volunteers continued to solve the difficult challenges, the language regions never lit up.***

This showed that people can indeed perform complicated tasks without needing to mutter to themselves in their heads!

### PSYCH TEST You Have Built-In Protection Against Hallucinations

Since your senses are imperfect, the brain has to find a way to separate reality from illusion. How does the brain achieve this?

- **a.** It slowly examines incoming information.
- **b.** It relies on memory to understand what is real or not.
- **c.** Any doubtful details are discarded.
- **d.** It keeps questioning what it knows.

## THIS BRAIN OVERLAP PLAYS WITH YOUR TONGUE

Sometimes, when kids are engrossed in a task, their tongues stick out. ***Some adults do the same, while others experience a more subtle version: pressing their tongue against the roof of their mouth.*** According to neuroscientists, this only happens when you need to do something delicate with your hands. The brain regions for tool use and dexterity overlap with the neural networks dedicated to language, so when you're fully focused on a motor task, it can tickle the language sector, which then engages the tongue, albeit a little strangely!

**PSYCH TEST** This Bias Created Planet Nine (Maybe)

In 2016, astronomers "discovered" Planet Nine based on the orbits of six distant rocks. Which bias could've created false data and an equally false planet?

a. Selection bias.
b. False hope syndrome.
c. Positivity bias.
d. Confirmation bias.

## ARGUING WITH YOURSELF DIVIDES YOUR BRAIN

The majority of people argue with themselves, some more than others! But have you ever wondered what it looks like in your brain when you start a squabble with yourself? ***Amazingly, the two hemispheres ping-pong, shifting between the left and right as you switch roles.*** In other words, when talking as the "you" that you're supporting, the left hemisphere lights up with a notably strong response in the auditory centers. When you switch to the "person" you're arguing with, brain activity shifts to the right hemisphere.

**PSYCH TEST** **More Reason to Guzzle $H_2O$**

The moment you feel thirsty, you're already dehydrated. But which cognitive effects does mild dehydration cause before you feel parched?

- **a.** Lower mood and inability to think clearly.
- **b.** A feeling of disconnect.
- **c.** A lower anger threshold.
- **d.** Inability to form durable long-term memories.

**RAPID ODDITY**

Sleep misperception is a brain phenomenon that makes you **think you're awake** when you're asleep.

## THE BIAS THAT WILL GET YOUR KIDS TO EAT THEIR BROCCOLI

Yes, that toddler who starts screaming the moment they see something green on their plate: We're talking about that kid! All right, this method isn't perfect, but researchers have found a bias in children that could make healthy eating easier. ***You simply give the child several choices but mention the chosen veggie last.*** Kids who are three or younger tend to echo the last option. It might not be the thing they want, but most toddlers aren't yet capable of the mental gymnastics required to remember and compare their choices before deciding.

## RAPID ODDITY

While engaged in a task that requires a lot of your working memory, you tend to **blink more**.

### THIS TRICK MAKES NARCISSISTS EXTRA SLIPPERY

***Also known as the "I knew it all along" bias, hindsight bias makes people view past events as more predictable than they really were.*** Someone with this bias might also overestimate how accurately they saw something coming, like the outcome of a sporting event or a political move.

In most cases, it's pretty harmless. But nothing stays cute and fuzzy when a narcissist adopts a bias, especially to escape accountability. People with narcissism use this bias not only to promote their own fantastic selves ("I knew this was going to happen all along") but also as an escape hatch when their predictions fall flat ("No one could've predicted that things were going to turn out this way!"). The latter is called "reverse hindsight."

But whether narcissists wield this bias "normally" or "in reverse," researchers argue that they have a stronger hindsight bias than most people. It serves their agenda of self-protection and self-enhancement very well. ***This deeply rooted bias is also the reason why most narcissists never learn from their mistakes or apologize for them.***

## RAPID ODDITY

A person's positive or negative **biases** can make the same cookie taste fresh or stale.

## RAPID ODDITY

**Neurocardiology** studies the cognitive links between the heart and the brain.

### APPRECIATING A GOOD TICKLE IS A BRAIN REFLEX

Thanks to an interview with Alicia Walf, a neuroscientist at Rensselaer Polytechnic Institute in New York, you can now follow the chain reaction behind the giddy sensations of tickling. When someone digs their fingers into your ribs, the skin's nerve endings send signals to the brain. These impulses then register in the somatosensory cortex, your brain's "physical sensations" center. Your limbic structures then help the brain to decide whether this feels good or annoying. ***If the brain finds it pleasant, it causes reflexive giggling.*** Interesting footnote: Laughing before someone has even tickled you is caused by anticipation!

**PSYCH TEST** Puzzle Over This

It's no secret that people love to solve challenges. But why are jigsaw puzzles in particular such a good activity for your brain?

a. Puzzles improve memory.
b. The activity enhances spatial coordination.
c. The activity disconnects the brain from daily worries.
d. Seeing colors makes the brain happy.

## RAPID ODDITY

Early childhood feelings, like shame or fear, often **fuel biases** and prejudiced behavior in adulthood.

**PSYCH TEST The Brain Treats Food and Socialness the Same**

The brain views eating and being social as very important. In what way does the brain treat these two activities the same to make them more appealing to you?

a. The brain creates cravings for both.
b. They both register as rewards in the brain.
c. The brain fades memories of bad friendships and food.
d. Your senses heighten when you see food or friends.

## YOU DON'T ACTUALLY HEAR MUSIC

On a neurological level, your sense of hearing is bizarre! Let's say you're a classy sort and you're listening to some classical music. What you're hearing starts out as nothing but sound waves. The brain takes these waves and translates them into electrochemical impulses. ***Amazingly, this switcheroo creates an image of the noise.*** This picture, so to speak, makes it easier for the brain to process the information so that it sounds like music. In truth, you don't hear any sounds. ***Instead, what you "hear" is an echo your mind constructed.***

**RAPID ODDITY**

Overcoming all of your biases is **almost impossible** because humans cannot truly achieve full objectivity.

## RAPID ODDITY

**What you perceive as the present is the brain's attempt to predict the next few seconds.**

### DAYDREAMING CAN BE A SLIPPERY SLOPE

Daydreaming can be fun. Experts have even discovered that it can enhance your ability to ease problems, depression, boredom, and pain. But because daydreaming is such a wonderful escape hatch from the world's problems, it can also become a compulsion. ***This is called "maladaptive daydreaming" and describes when you get lost in your head too much.*** Indeed, at the extreme end of the spectrum, some people attempt to avoid real life by living in their daydreams for hours at a time.

### PSYCH TEST This Brain Difference Sets Your Empathy Levels

Which neurons make some people empaths but could also contribute to the low empathy of malignant narcissists?

- a. Motor neurons.
- b. Mirror neurons.
- c. Hyperadaptive neurons.
- d. Memory neurons.

## RAPID ODDITY

Shuffling or dragging your feet could be a sign that your brain is **sleep-deprived**.

### YOUR BRAIN MISJUDGES RATTLESNAKES...LUCKILY!

For thousands of years, mammals have stepped on snakes. This is probably why rattlesnakes evolved their iconic tails—to shake a warning at approaching animals to avoid getting squashed. Researchers recently discovered that these reptiles don't just say, "Hey, I'm here!" ***They use different frequencies to make you believe they are closer than they really are.*** This trick is specifically aimed at mammal brains and is so well designed that you recognize the danger signal but not that it's an illusion. Let's be grateful that your noggin failed this one!

**PSYCH TEST** **The Brain's Mysterious Filter**

Visual information constantly shifts because of changes in viewpoint, light, and movement. How does the brain get rid of the chaos and present a stable world?

a. It keeps you in the past.
b. It ignores irrelevant information.
c. A specialized brain region stabilizes the chaos.
d. Most information gets quickly discarded as junk memories.

## RAPID ODDITY

Your brain builds an identity by **copying** the behaviors and mindsets of other people.

## CHAPTER 4

# COGNITIVE PSYCHOLOGY: MEMORY CREATION AND RECOLLECTION

Your memory is like a never-ending library. Several psychological processes—let's call them the librarians—flit around the brain, their arms full of newly acquired information. These busy beavers store images, feelings, and experiences at supersonic speed. When needed, they also run down to the cellar to retrieve an old memory or two.

But this well-oiled system is not flawless. Sometimes you forget things. False memories mimic the real deal, and let's not forget the sad events stored on the library's shelves. But that's where some of the most intriguing trivia tidbits are hiding—as you'll see in this chapter!

On the brighter side, you can also look forward to learning more about the dazzling abilities—and mysteries—of the brain when it comes to memory. These facts are guaranteed to turn you into an armchair cognitive psychologist (a classy bunch who gaze deeply into the mind to figure out how memories are created, recalled, and manipulated). But that's not all. The more you learn, the more you will understand why memory makes you unique and how, without it, you are basically a zombie. Indeed, without the ability to process, store, and retrieve information, you wouldn't be able to learn anything about the world or yourself!

This chapter will teach you a ton of fascinating stuff, like how to kill that earworm (finally), why doorways can wipe your mind, and how forgetfulness is a tonic for your long-term memory. Are you ready to step into your very own library and meet the pixies who guard your life story? Okay, so they often misplace files and forge the occasional image, but let's meet your memory bank as it is: brilliantly designed and full of surprises!

## THIS TECHNIQUE BESTED A FAMOUS GREEK MEMORY AID

The ancient Greeks had a brilliant way to boost memory. Think about an imaginary place, like a small room. Inside are objects. Attach the facts you need to recall to these items. When you need to remember, go back to this place and the objects will help you to remember the information you "stored" there. ***This highly effective technique is called the "mind palace technique."***

A recent study coauthored by David Reser used medical students to test this method against another ancient memory technique that has been used by countless generations of Australian Aborigines to pass down their history without writing anything down. It's similar to the mind palace technique in that information is also linked to something (in this case, a real place or object). And there's an extra perk: The teacher also tells a story.

Researchers aren't sure why students performed better when they used the Aboriginal technique. Perhaps being social had something to do with it. Traditionally, the Aboriginal method takes a group trip outdoors, but the students who tested the mind palace technique had to imagine a location on their own.

## MEET THE ELITE HSAM CREW

Those with highly superior autobiographical memory (HSAM) have perfect memory. ***Just ask them what they ate twelve years ago, and they'll name the time, date, place, napkin color, food, weather, and probably what conversation they were having and with whom.*** The condition is not appreciated by everyone. Merely seeing a date or image can trigger flashbacks of a particular day. This prompted Jill Price, one of the first people to be diagnosed with HSAM, to call the experience "uncontrollable, and totally exhausting."

Left-handed people often have a **better memory** than right-handed people.

**PSYCH TEST** Count Your Memories!

Long-term memory gets all the attention. But how many thoughts can you keep in your short-term memory and for how long?

**a.** Two or three for an hour.
**b.** Two to six for thirty minutes.
**c.** Seven for thirty seconds.
**d.** Twelve for six minutes.

## LOVE AT FIRST SIGHT? IT'S A MIND TRICK

You can blame Northwestern University for squashing your dreams of falling, Hollywood-style, for your partner the moment you meet. According to researchers, even if a person adores a stranger on sight and becomes romantically involved with them, the "love at first sight" experience is a false memory. In reality, as time goes by and the relationship deepens, subsequent feelings of love and new positive experiences travel back in time and project themselves onto the past, ***effectively tricking your memory into believing that the first meeting was mushier than it really was***.

## RAPID ODDITY

You recall only **20 percent** of what you hear and **30 percent** of what you see.

## HOW TO KILL AN EARWORM

If you are one of the lucky few who have never experienced this pesky phenomenon, an earworm is a melody that repeats in your mind. Earworms are surprisingly independent; they appear spontaneously and act beyond your control. So what triggers an earworm, and which bug spray do you need to get rid of it?

***Also known as "stuck song syndrome," this musical itch is a complicated process that involves several brain regions related to memory, emotions, perceptions, and spontaneous thoughts.*** A leading theory suggests that a wandering mind is fertile ground for earworms. The brain fills the empty, boring spaces by tapping into random memories—and sometimes music gets the stage. That's when your earworm grabs the mike and belts out the same six notes over and over.

The Zeigarnik effect is your bug spray. The mind created the worm, but it also doesn't appreciate incomplete things. The incessant looping could be a futile attempt on the brain's part to fix the fractured song. The Zeigarnik effect is all about closure. ***By consciously playing the song through to its end, you can satisfy the mind and smite the earworm.***

**PSYCH TEST Your Earliest Memories—Truth or Fiction?**

Many adults can recall events from when they were three years old and younger. But how reliable are these memories?

a. They are always reliable.
b. Very reliable—but only when the memories feel real.
c. Memories below the age of three are always false.
d. Your first memories are probably fictitious.

## HERE'S WHY YOU LOVE GOLDEN OLDIES

Nearly every generation prefers songs from its teenage years, but not necessarily because the music was better. ***The nostalgia might be linked to your "reminiscence bump," a time period that lasts from ages ten to thirty.*** According to psychologists, you disproportionately recall memories from this era, probably because it's filled with novel life experiences and intense feelings. Since music is closely linked to emotion and memory, it could explain why people prefer older tracks. The songs weren't necessarily superior; they were just seared into your mind with more emotion.

### PSYCH TEST Another Reason to Stand Up Straight

Good posture is important for physical health, but which positive benefit can it have on memory?

a. Better short-term memory recall.
b. Improved ability to remember happy memories.
c. Greater retention of complex information.
d. Remembering all memories more clearly.

## RAPID ODDITY

Exercise not only improves physical health but also **boosts your ability** to recall new information!

## SOME DOORS ARE AMNESIA PORTHOLES

Do you want your kid brother to forget a secret? Just tell him to walk through a doorway, and watch his memory vanish in a single, magical moment! If only. He's going to tattle to your parents, so let that one go. But there's a kernel of truth to this idea. ***What psychologists call the "doorway effect" can indeed snap its fingers and make you forget.***

Most people have gone into a room specifically to do something. But then, suddenly, their mind is an empty page. They cannot recall why they went in there, only that they had to do something or possibly fetch an item. This effect is so strong that you can even experience it in virtual reality.

Psychologists suspect that an open doorway, for some reason, creates a mental wall as soon as you enter a room. But how an architectural feature has the ability to wipe the human mind remains a mystery. The good news is that you're not losing your noodle. It's a commonplace event that one day, hopefully, will come with an equally fascinating explanation.

## YOUR NOSE REMEMBERS EVEN IF YOU FORGOT

You catch a whiff of something. Suddenly, out of the blue, a memory blossoms. You haven't thought about this place or person in years—and the emotions are surprisingly strong. None of the other senses provoke such vivid recollections. The reason? ***Smells reach the emotional and memory centers of the brain almost instantly, jumping a mere synapse or two.*** But any information from your eyes or ears first filters through the thalamus (a brain region), which prevents the same intimate connection with feelings and remembering.

## FETUSES HAVE MEMORY

Scientists at Queen's University of Belfast have unearthed evidence that supports something parents have always known: Unborn babies react to sounds. However, the studies also discovered that babies do not simply cartwheel when Mom plays a whale song and then forget about it. ***Weeks later, the fetuses recognize the same noises.***

An experiment in the Netherlands tested women in their final trimester, using a honking device on the babies. The results were amazing. When the fetuses heard the honking for the first time, they moved and their hearts began to beat faster. When exposed to the same sound ten minutes later, the babies had already figured out that the noise was harmless. This time, they didn't flail, nor did their heart rates spike. Those in their seventh month of gestation also recognized the same sound four weeks later. ***This learning ability to distinguish between scary new things and safe stimuli suggests that memory begins before you are born, albeit in a very rudimentary form.***

Interestingly, newborn babies continue to respond to any persistent sound they heard in the womb. For example, a study of mothers who regularly watched the same Spanish soap opera while pregnant found that their sprouts calmed down whenever the show's theme song played.

**PSYCH TEST** How to Create Durable Memories

Not all memories are created equal. Which emotional factor is responsible for creating the strongest, most durable memories?

a. Intense feelings, both negative and positive.
b. Only positive, strong feelings.
c. Deep focus.
d. A very interesting topic.

## YOU DIDN'T FORGET THAT PARTY

A drink-related blackout is a freaky thing. During the blackout, you are fully conscious and can hold a conversation. You can even walk around without spilling your fourteenth beer. But the next morning, you might wonder why you cannot remember the whole party. In reality, you never forgot anything. No memories were made during the blackout. ***When drinking too much or too fast, your blood alcohol level can spike to the point where it blocks the brain's ability to forge new memories.***

## GIVE SHORT-TERM MEMORY A GOLD STAR FOR LYING

One might be forgiven for thinking that the files in your long-term memory have a few missing pages and blurry information. After all, the passage of time is a great manipulator of reality. ***But, as it turns out, it's your short-term memory that needs to be taken with a pinch of salt.***

It might sound worrying, but this deception plays a critical role in how you perceive the world around you. When you take a second look at something, like an approaching car, the mind wants to confirm that the object is the same thing that you glanced at before, so your short-term memory slightly falsifies the second glance to match the first.

While this sounds insignificant, the alternative is bizarre. Without an altered second image, the brain would perceive the car as a totally new object because movement and changes in light altered its appearance and location. ***But thanks to your short-term memory's habit of superimposing one glance over the other, the mind knows it's the same car.***

A **single experience** can trigger both long-term and short-term memories but in different brain regions.

**PSYCH TEST Remembering Things That Never Happened**

Which engaging activity is fun but can also sometimes lead to the formation of false memories?

a. Watching movies.
b. Exploring fascinating topics.
c. Role-playing.
d. Reading good books.

## BRAIN BURPS

Imagine you run into a familiar face but cannot recall the person's name. While they talk a mile a minute, you desperately try to remember whether this is Bill or Bob. Afterward, you might worry. Is this the first sign of degenerative brain disease? According to neurologists, such blank moments are commonplace and necessary for the noggin to function normally. ***The brain has special neurons for forgetting, and their job is to take a broom and sweep away unnecessary fluff*** (like the names of old acquaintances). This keeps the brain's long-term storage uncluttered and healthy.

**RAPID ODDITY**

**False memories** can convince you that you're guilty of a crime you never committed.

## HOW TO ERASE PAINFUL MEMORIES 101

Painful baggage is such a widespread problem, especially with post-traumatic stress disorder (PTSD) and grief, that researchers want to find a way to rewrite the most haunting chapters of a person's story. Incredibly, they have discovered methods that can blunt traumatic recollections. Some, in theory, can even alter or delete memories.

Due to ethical reasons, scientists are hesitant to permanently erase parts of a person's mind. However, human trials involving norepinephrine-blocking drugs are promising. Stopping the release of norepinephrine, a chemical linked to the fight-or-flight response, can take the edge off memories that cause anguish.

***A process called "reconsolidation" also offers hope for those who'd rather tweak their bad memories without medication.*** Reconsolidation is the ability to change a memory during recall—and this is the loophole researchers want to exploit. Whenever you revisit a long-term memory, it becomes naturally impressionable. Your current state of mind can then change tiny details or, unfortunately, refresh the trauma. If therapists can guide a client to get their hands on a bad memory while it behaves like soft clay, then perhaps they can safely reshape it into something the client can live with.

**PSYCH TEST Your Memory's Filing Cabinet System**

In the past, researchers thought that memories were stored in one area of the brain. Where are they really stored?

- **a.** In the prefrontal cortex and hippocampus.
- **b.** In connections across the brain.
- **c.** Scientists aren't sure, but it's definitely not a single brain region.
- **d.** In the left hemisphere of the brain.

## RAPID ODDITY

To forget bad memories, some neuroscientists suggest that by **not resisting** them, they'll eventually fade.

## DO YOU HAVE EIDETIC OR PHOTOGRAPHIC MEMORY?

Many people have heard about eidetic and/or photographic memory. But how can you tell if you're among the lucky ones who have one or both? Well, you are lucky because everyone has eidetic memory! This is the ability to look at an object, close those eyelids, and see the object in your mind's eye. The image lingers only for a few seconds—but that's normal. Photographic memory is the long-term version. ***Few people have a true photographic memory, and, contrary to popular belief, these mental "photographs" aren't permanent; they last only for a few months.***

**PSYCH TEST** Get Artsy to Experience Super Memory

There are countless tricks to improve memory. Which simple, art-related tip is suggested by experts to remember almost anything?

a. Studying to classical music.
b. Doodling or drawing.
c. Creating a rhyme that holds the relevant information.
d. Painting the information (no matter how badly!).

## RAPID ODDITY

Korean-born babies adopted in the Netherlands couldn't, as adults, speak Korean, but their brains **recognized the language**.

## BAD MEMORY? TAKE UP PHOTOGRAPHY!

With a smartphone in nearly every hand, snapshots are at an all-time high. Indeed, in 2022, roughly 143 billion photos were taken every month. Naturally, memory experts sat up and took notice. There was a rumor swirling around that the constant photographing could turn humanity's memory to mush. After all, why store anything in your head when you can just get a picture of it on your phone?

Determined to discover what effects the constant selfies, food Instagrams, and vacation snaps had on the mind, scientists from New York University teamed up with three other universities. The researchers invited volunteers to a museum and divided them into two groups. Everyone was going to listen to an audio guide, but one group was asked to leave cameras and cell phones outside. Each volunteer in the other group could snap away to their heart's content.

***Interestingly, when the participants were later questioned about the exhibits, the shutterbugs had the best visual memory.*** It was almost as if their recall of specific moments was enhanced by the act of taking a picture. On the downside, they recalled fewer details about what they'd heard via the audio guide.

## HEALTHY SNACKS ARE HARD TO FIND—LITERALLY

Feel like a midnight snack? You're more likely to remember where you put the pizza leftovers than an apple. ***Called "optimal foraging theory," this refers to zooming in on high-calorie foods based on memory.*** Your ancestors needed such fare and ability when meals were scarce. However, according to a study published in *Scientific Reports*, this drive doesn't serve healthy eating today. Researchers released participants into a maze with food and later asked them about the locations of specific items. The volunteers mostly recalled where they found potato chips and chocolate but not healthy snacks.

### PSYCH TEST How "Brainy Bookmarks" Make Learning Easier

Which subconscious habit of the brain makes it easier for you to consciously learn about something new for the first time?

a. It gathers a lot of tiny details.
b. Exposure to new things primes the brain to learn about them later on.
c. It draws on any related information on the topic you already have.
d. It briefly experiences an increased learning ability for new things.

## RAPID ODDITY

Your brain can store and recognize between **five thousand and ten thousand** human faces.

## WHAT DAY IS IT?

Adults are expected to know what day of the week it is. But sometimes things get so hectic that you have to glance at your phone's calendar or whisper to an understanding friend, "Hey, is this Wednesday?" Upon hearing that it's really Thursday, most people are genuinely surprised about how they could've missed an entire day.

Let's get one worry out of the way! When calendar amnesia strikes, you're not alone. The University of Lincoln found that most people confuse one day for another—and frequently so. The researchers questioned almost 1,200 volunteers to gauge which day they thought it was and which feelings they associated with each day of the week. ***As it turned out, feelings had a lot to do with their ability to recall the correct day.***

A lot of the volunteers remembered Mondays and Fridays correctly. This was mainly due to Monday's famous reputation for being a sucky day, while Fridays are associated with emotions like freedom from work and looking forward to the weekend. But almost half of the participants got Tuesday, Wednesday, and Thursday muddled up because it "felt" like a different day.

**PSYCH TEST How Near-Identical Memories Stay Different**

Some memories are very similar. How does the brain differentiate among them to help you recall the right memory?

a. The brain fades one memory in favor of the other.
b. Small differences among memories are magnified.
c. Similar memories are stored in different areas of the brain.
d. The brain links similar memories to other, different stimuli.

## BORING MOMENTS LACK THIS MEMORY HORMONE

You've probably sat in a boring class and learned nothing. But you remember every detail about your surprise birthday party from six years ago. Despite the passage of time, you recall everything, from the jump scare to all the guests' faces. This memory bursts with color, sound, and motion. The same vivid memories are also formed during accidents and other unexpected events where surprise is a factor.

So why doesn't boredom have the same effect? According to MIT researchers, boredom just doesn't have the same biological ability as a surprise to sear memories into the brain. When your car suddenly skids on a wet road, the hormone norepinephrine floods the brain. The same thing happens in any situation where your system receives a sudden shock. ***Norepinephrine kicks several mental functions up a notch, including vigilance, attention, alertness, and learning.*** At that moment, when your brain is flooded with this chemical, lasting and rich memories are formed.

## DON'T RECALL YOUR BAD BEHAVIOR? YOU MIGHT HAVE ETHICAL AMNESIA!

When Harvard University put volunteers through their paces—nine studies, to be exact—the researchers concluded something interesting about morals. ***People are more likely to remember their own charitable acts than their own unethical behavior.*** Indeed, recalling how you swiped your sister's piggy bank challenges your moral self-concept to an uncomfortable degree. Researchers believe that this discomfort leads to "ethical amnesia" as you avoid bad memories in an attempt to believe that you are better-behaved than you really are. Such denial can even explain why some people continue to cheat or lie.

**PSYCH TEST** **And the Most Effective Reminder Is...?**

Sometimes, you forget mundane tasks, especially when you get distracted by other things. Which hack helps the brain to remember, and why?

a. An interesting reminder because it grabs the attention.
b. Any reminder, even boring ones, will jog the memory.
c. A written note because writing creates stronger memories.
d. A reminder on your phone because it's automatic.

## YOU HAVE AN AWESOME SENSE OF (MEMORY) STYLE!

A lot of arguments have been triggered by one thing, and that's when people recall the same event differently. In 2015, a groundbreaking study discovered that everyone's probably right. Sure, the whole family remembers the same wedding. ***But each person remembers different details and filters the day through their own perspective.*** The researchers found a biological basis for this. When volunteers answered questionnaires and sat in a brain scan while thinking about their past, their distinct brain connectivity patterns showed that people really do recall things in their own way.

### RAPID ODDITY

That **tip-of-the-tongue feeling**, when a memory is just out of reach, happens more when you're tired.

## RAPID ODDITY

The brain's capacity to store memories is big enough to hold the **entire Internet**.

### THE MYSTERY OF THE DREAMLESS DREAMERS

Why do some people fail to remember their dreams? There are different statistics on how many sleepers regularly recall their dreams, but roughly 6 percent claim to have no dreams at all. They either stopped dreaming years ago or never dreamed at all.

Sleep researchers in France decided to tackle this mystery in a novel way. They gathered 289 volunteers, about 2 percent of whom hadn't dreamed in over a decade and 1 percent who insisted that they'd never had a dream. Regardless of their claims, this particular group of sleepers was chosen because everyone had RBD (rapid eye movement behavior disorder).

Patients with this condition display physical movements during REM sleep, the stage when you dream. It gave the French team a way to monitor whether somebody was dreaming (or not) other than just taking their word for it.

While sleeping, some volunteers moved, shouted, and even talked. Upon awakening, the thrashers who "didn't dream" couldn't remember anything (as usual). ***But their behavior definitely suggests that even dreamless dreamers experience some sort of dream but, for some reason, form no memory of it.***

## RAPID ODDITY

The **context** in which memories are formed affects your ability to recall them later.

## DÉJÀ VU IS A MYSTERY (BUT IT MIGHT BE SPOTTY MEMORY)

For a long time, a moment of déjà vu (the uncanny feeling that you've been at a certain location before or a stranger looks freakishly familiar) was sidelined as a faulty brain moment, a neurological disorder, and even a paranormal experience. But these days, psychologists believe that it's normal and it has something to do with recognition and memory. The brain has two types of recognition memory: familiarity and recall. ***Déjà vu is likely linked to the familiarity side of things when you recognize a situation, location, or person, but the context is a little fuzzy.***

**PSYCH TEST** Elderly Forgetfulness Is Not What You Think

A common belief about aging is that it becomes harder to absorb new information, making you forgetful. But which mental process might actually be responsible?

a. A decline in interest.
b. Weakening short-term memory.
c. Taking in too much information.
d. Depression.

**RAPID ODDITY**

**Sleep spindles** (bursts of brain activity during sleep) can store memories and create false ones.

**PSYCH TEST** **You Might Not Be Real**

A person's identity is intimately linked to their life story. Which memory-related factor makes your history (and the person that you believe you are) a partial myth?

- **a.** You create false memories to fit your identity.
- **b.** Forgetting important memories that challenge your identity.
- **c.** Believing false statements from others about yourself.
- **d.** You lie to others about yourself, giving them false memories.

**RAPID ODDITY**

Some people with amnesia don't remember they just had lunch and will **immediately eat again**.

## LET'S TALK ABOUT YOUR HEDONISTIC YOUTH

Many people recall their younger years as one big party. Some undoubtedly passed out on the dance floor once or twice (or a few dozen times). But in most cases, this wild child narrative is not the whole story. ***During your teens and twenties, novel experiences abound, and they create strong memories.*** Your "party days" also had lots of dreary chores, schoolwork, and events that didn't excite you. But whenever something fun happened, your brain scorched the experience into your memory. This is why, when you reminisce about your youth, most memories stay hazy except for the good times.

**PSYCH TEST How Full Is Your Brain?**

The brain's capacity to store information is amazing. But why can the brain never be truly "full"?

a. New information-storing connections form all the time.
b. The removal of short-term memories keeps the brain from getting full.
c. Old information is pushed out.
d. Older memories fade to make more space.

## THE MANDELA EFFECT ISN'T AS SPOOKY AS YOU THINK

For those who are not familiar with this effect, here's a quick introduction. Former South African president Nelson Mandela died in 2013. This surprised a lot of people who were convinced that they saw his funeral on TV—in the eighties. The Internet community found similar events and reasoned that we're experiencing parallel time lines or that our world is a glitch-ridden simulation.

It's fun to imagine that we're witnessing wrinkles in time or that we're inside an alien computer game. But the truth is more mundane. ***The Mandela effect is caused by groupthink and misinformation.*** In Mandela's case, another prominent figure (who belonged to Mandela's political party) passed away in South Africa in 1977, and this death received a lot of media attention. It's possible that this event caused the later mass "recollection" that it was Mandela's funeral being shown on TV.

A closer look at other "Mandela cases" usually exposes them as myths too. But despite this, people are adamant that they remember things correctly even though it's all a case of widespread Internet misinformation and how people tend to forgo fact-checking when things really intrigue them.

## LET'S CHAT ABOUT MEMORIES

Sharing a memory or reminiscing together with loved ones feels great. ***But when you look under the hood of this simple pastime, the benefits are surprising, both in number and purpose.*** To start with, sharing difficult memories can lighten the load and facilitate healing. Sharing positive and informative moments, on the other hand, can help people bond and catch up on news.

Reminiscing is also advantageous for a group, whether it's a circle of friends or a family. It serves to debrief others, people learn more about each other, and it maintains a group's shared identity. But don't worry: Your own identity won't get lost! Research shows that sharing memories within a group also helps to preserve the identities of individuals.

The magic doesn't end there. ***Sharing a story from the past—or retelling a tale—plays a critical role in the psychological development of young children and older people.*** Learning more about their family gives children a sense of who they are and where they come from. Elderly couples who reminisce together also tend to remember the best moments of their life in greater detail than older adults who do so alone.

**PSYCH TEST Combat and Memory**

Violent trauma causes memory impairment. But how quickly can physical combat harm the memories of those involved?

a. Instantly.
b. One minute.
c. Fifteen minutes.
d. About half an hour.

## FORGIVENESS CAN MAKE YOU FORGET

We've all heard the old adage "forgive and forget." But it might be more accurate to say, "forgive *to* forget." Indeed, one of the main reasons people cannot let go of painful memories caused by betrayal is because they keep picking at these memories. ***Rumination keeps the events fresh in your mind and thus prevents healing.*** Studies from the University of St. Andrews have shown that forgiving can dramatically decrease the number of times you revisit a painful memory. Starved of attention, the memory and all the feelings associated with it begin to fade.

### RAPID ODDITY

**Flashbacks** are distressing memories that enter a person's consciousness instantly and involuntarily.

## HERE'S WHY YOUR MEMORY IS WONKY AFTER SURGERY

Without anesthetics, critical operations wouldn't be possible. Anesthesia's purpose is to induce a pain-free coma and cause memory loss (it switches on the brain's "amnesia" receptors). This amnesia is supposed to prevent patients from remembering only what happened during the surgery, but one-third of all patients suffer from impaired memory for months afterward. Eventually, Canadian scientists discovered why. Normally, when the drugs leave the system, the amnesia receptors turn off. ***But for some reason, for the unlucky one-third, these receptors stay active when the drugs wear off.***

## RAPID ODDITY

Vitamin D can improve memory, but taking too much can **slow down** your physical reactions.

### THIS MEMORY SMILED FOR THE CAMERA

In 2009, the University of California proved something that scientists had only suspected for years: ***Long-term memories are "born" when new proteins form at connections between brain cells.*** Researchers turned to the humble sea slug because the animal's brain cells are a good model for those of humans. Before turning on the cameras, they dosed the critter with a fluorescent protein and serotonin (to stimulate memory formation). Nobody knows what the slug was thinking, but when bright new proteins started popping up, the world got its first image of a memory being formed!

**PSYCH TEST** Try This Fun Memory Aid

There are many memory techniques, but which natural, social behavior can also improve your memory?

a. Eating and drinking with a group.
b. Texting a friend.
c. Talking to another person.
d. Going for a group walk.

## RAPID ODDITY

Your brain can recognize certain songs after hearing just **one second** of music.

## RAPID ODDITY

Breathing through the nose **right after** smelling new scents helps you to remember them better.

### DID A NARCISSIST FORGET YOUR NAME? IT'S KIND OF NORMAL (FOR THEM)

Imagine that you bump into the local narcissist. You've met this person before and so greet them by name. But when it's their turn to say your name, all you get is a confused look. For once, they're not trying to hurt you by "forgetting" who you are. ***According to psychologists, this personality type struggles with name recall.*** The reason is simple. People with healthy relationships have the ability to quickly associate names with faces. But narcissists are so preoccupied with themselves that they often fail to process the simplest information about others.

**PSYCH TEST** Memories Can Help with Panic Attacks

A panic attack is a strong beast that is hard to stop. But which type of memory can sometimes stop a panic attack?

a. Thinking about a calming place.
b. Recalling a completely accepting friend.
c. Remembering a joke.
d. Following a guided meditation you memorized.

## RAPID ODDITY

By merely **inhaling** the aroma of coffee, you can improve your memory and attention span.

## THE VIRUS BEHIND YOUR MEMORY

Meet Arc. ***This tiny protein gives you the ability to learn and store long-term memories.*** Without Arc, humans wouldn't be humans. Naturally, researchers wanted to take a closer look at this important little guy, and boy, were they in for a few surprises. The first revealed that Arc had evolved millions of years ago. This ancient protein also has properties that are very similar to what viruses use to infect cells. In fact, under a microscope, Arc resembles the retrovirus HIV.

***The most shocking discovery was that it also acts like a virus.*** A real virus spreads inside a host by copying its own genetic material, and, after infecting a healthy cell, it repeats the process with neighboring cells. During several experiments, Arc was tested for this viral trademark, and the results floored the researchers. Arc had a type of capsid, which is the package that viruses use to float their genetics to the next cell. The protein filled these capsids with its mRNA and, in true virus fashion, transferred its genetics in a chain reaction from one brain cell to the next.

## SAD FACES REMEMBER OTHER FACES

Forget about mugging someone who looks blue. According to science, sad individuals are more likely to pick you out in a lineup. This discovery was made when scientists in 2012 put students in a good mood by playing upbeat music. They also depressed a second group with tragic tunes. Everyone was shown thirty-two images of faces and then given a brief break. The original images were then added to an equal number of new faces. When the students were asked to recall as many of the originals as they could, ***the sad students outperformed the happy crowd***.

## THE BRAIN'S MYSTERIOUS MAPS

Sometimes, the simplest riddles can be the toughest nuts to crack. In this case, researchers still don't know how you remember where you are going, like finding your way to the cheese aisle or traveling by car to another town. ***They do know that the brain creates maps using complex calculations and sensory feedback.*** Once this map is filed away in your memory, finding the Cheddar on your second trip will be a breeze. Scientists have also identified the parietal cortex as your personal mapmaker, but how it manages this feat remains a mystery.

**PSYCH TEST** **How to Sacrifice Memory for Memory**

Which popular memory technique improves your intake of information but makes remembering a little scratchy?

a. Repetition learning.
b. Using flash cards.
c. The mind palace technique.
d. Listening to a recorded lesson.

### RAPID ODDITY

**Retrograde amnesia** steals your old memories, while anterograde amnesia stops new ones from forming.

## RAPID ODDITY

You can remember things **more accurately** when you close your eyes.

## ARE YOU A GRAND MASTER?

***Many titles honor people with big brains, but one prestigious moniker is the Grand Master of Memory.*** The World Memory Sports Council first bestowed this crown upon a brainy individual in 1995 after they aced the necessary trials. Until 2013, to become a Grand Master, you had to memorize a deck of cards within two minutes, ten decks in an hour, and one thousand numbers in an hour. These days, you must enter a World Memory Championship, earn five thousand points, and finish among the top five competitors to win the title.

### PSYCH TEST The Strange Way You Remember

Your brain memorizes what you see by absorbing the details first and then looking at the bigger picture. But what happens during recall?

a. The brain reverses the process.
b. The brain instantly retrieves the whole memory.
c. The brain merges the memory with similar memories.
d. Only fragments of the memory are remembered.

**PSYCH TEST Sugar Can Shock Your Memory**

A candy bar won't zing your brain, but during septic shock, how does sugar affect the brain so severely that it causes memory loss?

a. It significantly slows down brain functions.
b. It prevents the formation of new memories.
c. It disrupts connections in the hippocampus.
d. Septic shock allows sugar to flood the entire brain.

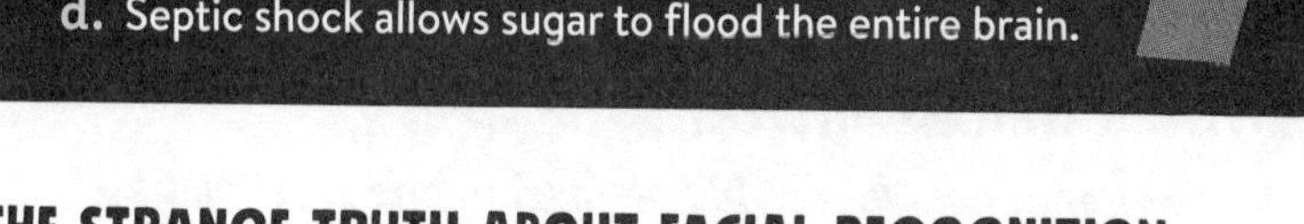

## THE STRANGE TRUTH ABOUT FACIAL RECOGNITION

We all have that one friend who never forgets a face. Perhaps you are that person! Either way, if someone asked where in the brain this skill is lodged, you might answer, "Why, in my long-term memory, of course." Wrong. ***The bizarre truth is that your ability to always remember a face comes from your short-term memory.***

In the depths of your short-term memory is a special room just for images: VSTM (visual short-term memory). Researchers have likened its ability to store faces to a suitcase. The amount of stuff that you can cram into a bag depends on how well you pack the items. Similarly, VSTM is an expert in packaging faces.

VSTM is primed to recognize faces more than other objects and images, probably because social interactions remain an important part of being human. But the system is not automatic. ***You need to look at a face for at least four seconds to store it.*** Glancing at a passerby for a millisecond will not leave a lasting impression on your VSTM.

**RAPID ODDITY**

Forgetting burns **more brain power** than remembering.

## RAPID ODDITY

You can distinguish among **millions of colors**, but your brain struggles to remember specific shades.

## LIGHT SLEEPERS ARE DREAM MAESTROS

Some people remember their dreams in technicolor. Others have to be satisfied with vague images and feelings—or even a totally blank screen. Researchers stumbled across an interesting difference between these two groups. Those who struggle with dream recall tend to snooze more deeply and for longer periods of time throughout the night. ***Individuals who frequently remember their dreams, however, wake up more often.*** Since you are more likely to remember a dream right after you wake up, it could explain why heavy sleepers tend to forget their dreams.

**PSYCH TEST** Old Memories Leave Echoes

All memories fade with time, even durable ones. Which part of a memory tends to remain after its other details are lost?

- **a.** Only the most important part, or "gist."
- **b.** The most emotional part.
- **c.** Small details and colors.
- **d.** The feelings and hazy visuals.

## RAPID ODDITY

Anticipating a stressful day in the morning can **weaken your memory** throughout that day.

## CHAPTER 5

# PERSONALITY PSYCHOLOGY: A GUIDE TO UNDERSTANDING YOUR EMOTIONS

See that scary-looking guy holding an ax? The shiver of fear running through your body is correct to suggest that now is *not* a good time to poke your finger in his eye. Emotions are like that. While they can make you do questionable things (hey, this eye prank might be funny...), they also keep you safe (...let's put some distance between you and that blade).

Indeed, emotions are not just feelings: They are complex mental and physiological responses that govern your decisions, actions, and outlook on life. They also continuously craft a unique personality for every one of the almost eight billion people alive today—and everyone who has ever lived!

That's interesting and all, but how does learning about emotions benefit you? Well, personality psychology gives you the tools to understand human nature by looking at feelings, behaviors, and thought patterns. Even if you have no interest in chasing a psychology degree, understanding how feelings work can promote emotional intelligence, more control over unhealthy habits, and better relationships with others.

In this chapter, you'll discover all kinds of fascinating trivia related to the blues, joy, and everything in between—like why love is not an emotion (maybe), how you can cry someone else's tears, and why flowers make your brain swoon. Are you ready to discover how your emotions play a major role in psychology? Let's dive in!

## HANGER IS NOT JUST ABOUT HUNGER

The word "hangry" refers to the crabbiness a person feels because they're hungry. In 2018, scientists discovered that the popular explanation for hanger was not entirely correct. ***As it turns out, when a person feels irritated because they skipped a meal, it's not just the hunger pangs that trigger their short fuse.***

The researchers were a little sneaky with this experiment. They gathered volunteers who had no idea that the experiment was designed to provoke hanger. Some students were asked to fast for five hours beforehand, and, to irritate their hungry nerves, they were given a complicated digital assignment that took hours to complete. The computer was also programmed to crash on purpose—right before they finished.

The results revealed the side of hanger that was to be expected: Those who hadn't eaten experienced anger—even hatred—when the scientists "blamed" them for the computer crash. But other hungry participants, who were asked to think about their emotions before reporting their feelings, showed less irritation despite being told that the crash was their fault. ***This suggests that hanger is a complex mix of needing a granola bar, personality, and environmental influences.***

## RAPID ODDITY

A team from the University of Glasgow acknowledges only **four basic emotions:** happiness, sadness, fear, and anger.

## RAPID ODDITY

**Laughter** temporarily steamrollers other emotions. You can't sob or feel rage while chuckling!

## HANGXIETY IS A THING TOO!

Hangovers suck. It's bad enough when you get symptoms like torturous headaches, nausea, and fatigue. But roughly 12 percent of people also suffer from persistent anxiety during a hangover, or "hangxiety." Anyone can experience a nervy hangover. But after studying partygoers, researchers identified those who are more susceptible. People with shy personalities, those who "catastrophize" pain, individuals who feel guilty about drinking, and those with stressful lives are all more likely to develop hangxiety. ***Due to their preexisting vulnerability to negative emotions, the fallout of a hangover hits them extra hard.***

### PSYCH TEST Skip the Urge to Comfort-Smile

Most parents, in an attempt to spare their children pain, put on a "happy face" during hard times. But which negative effects does this have on the parent?

a. Reduced well-being and a lower-quality bond with the child.
b. Depression and pent-up anger.
c. Secretly resenting the child, their spouse, or both.
d. Increased levels of anxiety and loneliness.

## HUMOR? CHOCOLATE? SAME THING

Not everyone finds the same joke amusing. ***But in general, the secret ingredient to laughter is the good old switcheroo: Your brain expects one thing, but, a few words later, that assumption is blown out of the water.*** A 2003 study wanted to know more—specifically, how the brain reacts to humor. When researchers scanned volunteers watching funny cartoons, they found that chucklesome moments ran deliciously deep. Whenever the participants felt humor, it lit up the same pleasure sensors that sparkle when people enjoy chocolate.

## WHY REJECTION HITS LIKE A TRUCK

Anyone who's been through an unwanted breakup might've noticed something peculiar. Nobody is beating you with a stick, but you're physically hurting. How is this possible when the experience is an emotional one? Yeah, you can blame your ancestors for that one (not your grandma: your hunter-gatherer cousin).

Back in the day, social rejection was no laughing matter. It could get you killed. Without the protection of a tribe, nobody would rescue you from danger, hand you a tasty root when food got scarce, or help you carry your genes into the next generation.

These days, people are less dependent on others to eat, to stay warm, or even to have families. But there's no escaping how much the brain still fears social rejection. ***Biologically speaking, rejection mimics physical agony—the brain cannot tell the difference.*** So, to warn you of this "threat," it zings you with unpleasant sensations. As a result, when your crush tears up that Valentine's Day card, you feel the loss pushing down on your chest, while sorrow, humiliation, and anxiety creep across your skin and stomach.

## RAPID ODDITY

**Ellipsism** is the sad realization that you won't live to see the future.

## SAD FEELINGS NEED A GOOD SHOWER

Psychologists have always wondered why people cry it out in the shower. What makes the bathroom so attractive that the "shower cry" is actually a thing? It's not easy to study people in the shower (without getting arrested), but when researchers combed through data that detailed the crying habits of 5,096 people in thirty-five countries, they realized that most preferred to cry at home alone. ***The shower is perfect: It's at home and it offers total privacy.*** The soothing sensation of running water might also lure weepy willows to the bathroom.

**PSYCH TEST There Are Two Green-Eyed Monsters**

Envy and jealousy are very similar. But which negative belief sits at the root of jealousy that makes it different?

- **a.** That you own something or someone.
- **b.** Low self-worth.
- **c.** A perceived threat to something you value, real or imagined.
- **d.** The fear of being alone or shortchanged.

## RAPID ODDITY

Anger is a **secondary emotion**; it is a symptom of other emotions like fear, irritation, or frustration.

## HOW TO SPOT A REAL SMILE

Since the dawn of time, humans have been grinning at each other. It shows joy during reunions, appreciation for kindness, and more. But the smile can also be a mask designed to distract others from a person's true intentions or emotions. To the untrained eye, saccharine smiles and a genuine grin both look the same. However, there is a biological signal that can help you to spot the real deal!

A heartfelt smile is spontaneous. It can happen quicker than a thought, but fake grins can also appear in an instant, so it's not about the speed. It's about the eyes. During the 1800s, French scientist Guillaume Duchenne was the first to realize that smiling engaged two groups of facial muscles. The first, the zygomaticus major muscles, tug at the corners of the mouth, and people can control them at will. The second group, the orbicularis oculi, lines the area around the eyes and is involuntary. ***So when someone beams at you and the eyes are crinkled at the corners, you're looking at a so-called Duchenne smile—a.k.a. a genuine smile.***

**PSYCH TEST** Tears Are Natural Tranquilizers

The emotions leading up to weeping are often horrible. Why does a good cry turn things around with feelings of calmness?

a. It is physically exhausting.
b. It releases feel-good hormones.
c. It gets rid of stress hormones while also releasing feel-good hormones.
d. Most people cry at night in bed when they're sleepy anyway.

## ANGRY FINGERS AND STEERING WHEELS DON'T GEL

Do you regularly white-knuckle your way through traffic? This might not be the best survival strategy. In one of the largest studies to ever analyze traffic accidents, researchers in the US observed drivers and noticed a disturbing trend. ***Those behind the wheel who were noticeably in the grip of road rage or who appeared otherwise irritated or sad or who were crying were ten times as likely to have an accident.*** Distraction was also a huge evil, and one particular activity—driving while dialing a number—increased someone's odds of an accident by twelve times.

### RAPID ODDITY

One in ten people have **alexithymia**, or a difficulty expressing or identifying with emotions.

## LOVE IS NOT AN EMOTION...OR IS IT?

Imagine being told that love is not an emotion but a physiological response (like hunger or feeling sleepy). Most people would disagree. Love is almost universally accepted as a heartfelt emotion that is shared between romantic partners, family, and friends. The public stands firm behind Cupid, but psychologists are not so unified. ***Some experts point to solid evidence that love is just a blend of biological drivers and feelings of attachment.*** But others, while accepting of the hormones and physical responses, insist that love is also a very complex emotion.

RAPID ODDITY

People are more attracted to **hearty, open-mouthed laughter** than closed-mouthed or snorting laughs.

## FLOWERS MAKE YOUR BRAIN HAPPY

Your brain is a flower freak. Indeed, scientists have discovered that the happiness people feel when they receive a bouquet or hike through wildflowers is not skin-deep. ***In the presence of petals, the brain oozes three powerful "happiness" chemicals: dopamine, oxytocin, and serotonin.***

This reaction is not really strange, considering how culturally significant flowers have been to humans for thousands of years. You no longer look at blooms the same way your ancestors probably did (as important harbingers of harvests and the end of harsh winters, for example), but flowers still trigger the same psychological processes. These, in turn, release each of the three chemicals.

Dopamine is tied to rewards, which could be why bouquets remain a traditional gift for champions on the Olympic podium. Flowers from a lover might release oxytocin, the "bonding hormone," which builds social trust and deeper relationships. Similarly, the release of serotonin can make a person feel more important. Together, this heady cocktail makes the brain more trusting and happier. So, the next time you want to buzz a loved one with a natural high, gift them a flowering plant!

## SCREAMING: NOT JUST NOISE

A yell seems simple enough, but scream researchers (they really exist) have discovered that ***humans convey a lot of emotions this way***. A welcome surprise might warrant a loud squeal. Road rage causes shouting. But screams of terror can freeze other people in their tracks. Upon hearing a wail of fear, you become fully focused on the person or the direction the sound came from. This visceral fascination is probably a legacy left by generations of ancestors who survived because they screamed or listened to the urgency of this danger signal.

## ARE YOU TOXICALLY PERKY?

Looking back through history, positivity was not always important and the individual was not as valued as the group. These days, positivity slogans are everywhere. People are encouraged to celebrate themselves as unique, upbeat go-getters. You know, the type who soars on the wings of endless positivity.

And therein lies the problem. Contrary to what self-help gurus claim, positivity cannot be a constant state of mind, nor should it be.

There is inherently nothing wrong with feeling great. When happiness and confidence are genuine, you're experiencing life in a healthy way. The problem starts when negative emotions arise and you sweep the pain under the carpet with a good attitude. This is fine once or twice, but not every time you feel bad.

***Toxic perkiness is an avoidance strategy.*** People force feelings of happiness to avoid dealing with rejection, fear, or sadness. Well-meaning but hapless friends can also tap into toxic positivity to mute a loved one's pain. Instead of giving helpful advice, they'll rely on empty comforts like "It could've been worse," "At least you still have your health," "Just stay positive," and so on.

**PSYCH TEST The Bright Side of Disgust**

Disgust is not the best emotion to experience, but which positive purpose do feelings of revulsion serve?

- **a.** It keeps you safe from potentially dangerous things.
- **b.** It is a nonverbal way to communicate dislike to others.
- **c.** It reinforces existing fears.
- **d.** It encourages conflict avoidance.

## YOU CAN CRY SOMEONE ELSE'S TEARS

When someone yawns, it can set off a chain reaction of yawns around the room. But did you know that emotions are also contagious? This holds true for both negative and positive responses. You often tear up when a loved one cries, and laugh when friends find something funny.

But how do emotions jump between people? More importantly, what purpose does it serve? Remarkably, this process, which researchers from the University of Twente in the Netherlands call "emotional contagion," is a spontaneous occurrence. It feels so natural that neither the spreader nor the catcher realizes what is happening. Scientists from the University of Chicago even pointed out that when you catch someone else's emotions, the muscle fibers in your body and face activate on their own to mimic what the other person is feeling. Although this response is also incredibly subtle, the muscle reaction is what triggers the same emotion in your brain.

Sometimes, you can catch the emotions of a close friend's friend who heard a sad story about another friend. So why do people borrow sorrow? ***Simply put, sharing happy news or showing support during grief can build better social bonds—something your cave person brain craves.***

## INTROVERSION IS NOT AN EVOLUTIONARY BLOOPER

All students of psychology eventually come to understand that the brain is hardwired to be social. This harks back to ancient times when getting along with other cave folk meant the difference between life and death. For this reason, logic might conjure an image of the most successful people sitting around a campfire every night, clinking together their stone cups and bonding. Any introverts sitting to one side might slowly dehydrate and starve...right? Things are never that simple with the brain. Introverts, with their quiet and cautious nature, are not an evolutionary mistake.

***Both personality types were crucial for humanity's survival, and they still are.*** Neurological and genetic research shows that extroverts are rewarded with dopamine when they interact with others or take risks. Their adventurous nature came in handy when people had to work together to hunt a mammoth or explore new food sources. However, running after dangerous animals and testing that new, enticing berry also increased the odds of an ancient extrovert having a short life. The less impulsive introverts, on the other hand, were more likely to survive in the long run.

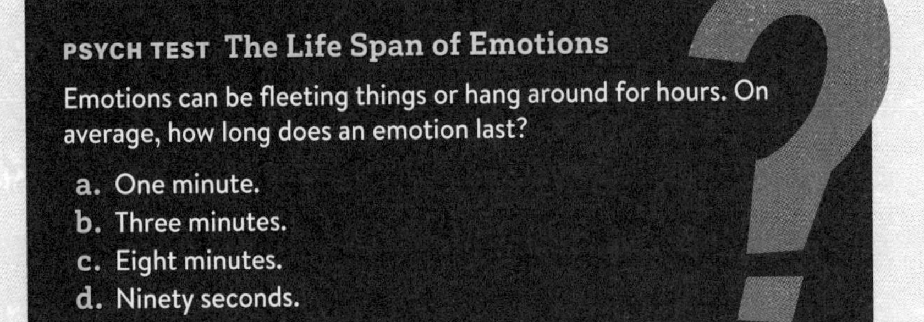

**PSYCH TEST** **The Life Span of Emotions**

Emotions can be fleeting things or hang around for hours. On average, how long does an emotion last?

- **a.** One minute.
- **b.** Three minutes.
- **c.** Eight minutes.
- **d.** Ninety seconds.

## RAPID ODDITY

**Sleep deprivation** interferes with your ability to read other people's emotions.

## DO FUN STRANGERS FRUSTRATE YOU? THERE'S A REASON FOR THAT

Frustration with friends usually has to do with toxic behavior or that pal who always borrows money. Then there is adronitis. ***This emotion strikes when you meet a new person and they're so fascinating it's frustrating.*** The new friend isn't doing anything wrong. But their magnetism fuels your desire to fully experience—as in, right now—what they have to offer. However, at the same time, you know this isn't possible because it takes time to get to know someone. These conflicting feelings are guaranteed to give you a good dose of adronitis!

### PSYCH TEST New Grandparents Pluck This Nerve

After the birth of a child, new parents can experience sadness and anger toward their own parents. Choose the reason why this happens.

a. Loving their child reminds parents of the missing love in their own childhood.
b. As the caregivers for their parents and children, new parents feel burdened.
c. Seeing the elderly reminds them that their baby, too, will grow old.
d. Grandparents often interfere with new parents' parenting styles.

## A SONG THAT FIGHTS SEIZURES

Something curious happened in 1993. ***Scientists discovered that people can develop better spatial reasoning abilities after listening to the music of Mozart for ten minutes.*** This became known as the "Mozart effect."

More recently, a group of researchers was looking for a noninvasive way to treat epilepsy that cannot be controlled with medication. Taking a chance with the Mozart effect, they played Mozart's *Sonata for Two Pianos in D Major K. 448* to sixteen patients who had uncontrollable epilepsy and IEDs, which are short, harmful brain events that occur between seizures.

In 2021, the study published a remarkable discovery. After patients listened to the sonata for thirty seconds, their IED events decreased. The song's longer musical phrases (those that lasted more than ten seconds) were even more beneficial.

This soothing influence is not fully understood, but the mystery seems to have something to do with the longer pieces and the emotions they provoke. ***During the experiment, the music was reported to have created a sense of anticipation followed by surprise.*** This combination triggered positive emotional reactions in the patients. Again, why this worked, nobody knows.

## USE TURTLE THINK

Modern culture can pressure people to make important decisions without delay. Needless to say, this is not only stressful; it can also lead to mistakes. Researchers discovered that the elderly tend to make the best decisions, partially because of their life experiences but also because they know the value of Turtle Think, which is ***the slow consideration of one's choices before making a final decision***. The study also showed that slow thinkers are better at recognizing relevant information, leading to good decision-making more often.

**PSYCH TEST** **What Really Makes Busy Bees Happy?**

Boredom can lead to negative feelings, but so can a busy day at the office. What small emotional difference can make busy people happier?

a. The expectation of a financial reward.
b. Setting an intention to stay focused on the present moment.
c. Enjoying tasks that are meaningful.
d. The support from others working on the same project.

**RAPID ODDITY**

Listening to sad songs can provoke **positive emotions** like nostalgia, wonder, and peacefulness.

## ARE YOU A LIBRA? PROBABLY NOT

It's fun to belong to a zodiac sign. But researchers aren't always a fun bunch. They set out to prove, once and for all, that astrology doesn't influence personality. ***During a 2003 review of several studies, professional astrologers were ousted when their results were shown to be no more accurate than chance.*** Another large study involving 173,709 volunteers also determined that their birth signs didn't influence their personalities, even among the believers. Speaking of believers, some don't need evidence either way. They have faith in the zodiac and stay quite attached to their personal sign!

## SECRETS ARE MEH FOR YOUR MENTAL HEALTH

Let's say your best friend tells you a secret—and not a good one. On the one hand, secrets can give people a sense of power and even put a chip on their shoulder. It's that "I know something you don't" thing. These are the smug keepers of the Untold. But most secrets prey on your emotions like a parasite, leaching positivity and leaving anxiety and even depression in its place. ***Keeping secrets can even lead to poor health.***

It's not just the hairy content of a secret that grates on emotions. ***Humans are wired to share intense information, and this is why secret-keeping is a skill that most people suck at.*** The very effort to go on with your day and not disclose your burden has been known to drive some people to self-medicate and try other harmful behaviors.

So, if the end result is a damaged friend or family member, why do people share secrets with others? Trusting someone with a secret not only strengthens social bonds (mostly); it also gives the person telling the secret a welcome break from constantly guarding the information.

**PSYCH TEST** **When You're More Than Homesick**

Some people don't just miss an old house or their home country; they feel like their soul was left behind. Choose the most detrimental drawback of this grief.

- **a.** A normal life but increased depression.
- **b.** Feeling hatred toward your new town or country.
- **c.** You are mentally and emotionally trapped in your past.
- **d.** Seeking relief in harmful substances or activities.

## RAPID ODDITY

The cozy feeling of being indoors during a rainstorm is called "**chrysalism**."

## WHY DATE NIGHT NEEDS NOSTALGIA

A fancy dinner is nice, but you need to roll up your sleeves and do something more if you want a lasting romantic relationship. According to researchers, a good move is to shower your partner with nostalgia. This emotion, which is basically feeling sentimental about the past, ***can strengthen two important things for couples: relationship satisfaction and commitment***. However, it's not enough to relate a story of how you went swimming as a child and accidentally inhaled a tadpole. The trick is to reminisce over experiences that you have shared with your partner.

**PSYCH TEST** **Why Friend Breakups Hit Like a Hammer**

For some, "breaking up" with a friend is more shattering than losing a romantic partner. Choose the emotion-related reason behind this phenomenon.

a. It triggers disenfranchised grief.
b. You regret the time and energy invested in that friend.
c. There's a lot of unresolved hurt.
d. You feel betrayed or cast aside.

## RAPID ODDITY

In some cases, when people feel excited or anxious, they **get hiccups**.

## RAPID ODDITY

**"Opia" describes the invasive arousal you feel when making long, direct eye contact with someone.**

## PEOPLE BOND WITH BUILDINGS

Humans possess an unusual tendency to feel strong feelings—even love—for buildings, statues, and landmarks. This might seem strange, considering that none are living things. However, the emotional attachment is real enough, and ***people feel pain for neglected places and devastation when a structure they're fond of gets the demolition treatment***. Indeed, social psychologists know that people who have bonded with doomed buildings can be badly affected by the loss. This sense of loss can trigger grief and even wound the identity of the individual or the collective well-being of a community.

### PSYCH TEST When the Calmness Is Callous

Paradoxical anxiety is when an attempt to relax makes you more anxious. Why does this happen?

- **a.** Turning one's focus inward is unsettling.
- **b.** Relaxing steals time from work and responsibilities.
- **c.** The boredom triggers anxiety.
- **d.** You struggle to relax and feel anxious about it.

**PSYCH TEST** **Meet Your First Feelings**

Primary affects are the earliest emotions you experience. How many such "first" feelings do some experts believe you have?

a. Four.
b. Seven.
c. Nine.
d. Ten.

## THE EMOTIONAL ORACLE EFFECT

Here's another good reason not to bury your feelings. According to an article in the *Journal of Consumer Research*, eight studies have discovered a fascinating ability, one that is unique to people who trust their own emotions. Just like the legendary psychic oracles, ***they can predict the outcomes of future situations better than those who doubt or suppress their own feelings***. However, this ability needs some background experience in a particular topic—like predicting the weather because you're a meteorologist. But despite this knowledge, the effect stands. If you're an expert in your field but doubt your feelings, the accuracy of your forecasts is likely to drop.

## RAPID ODDITY

Adults experience **liberosis** when life's worries make them miss the carefree days of their childhood.

## RAPID ODDITY

**Anticipatory anxiety** occurs when you creep yourself out by fearing a danger that isn't present.

### FAKE FEAR IS SCARY TOO

There's a sentiment floating around in the world of neuroscience... and it's not very flattering. But the gist is that people are probably the most fearful species on the planet—not turkeys in the week leading up to Thanksgiving. Nope, the Nervous Nellies of Earth are humans. To understand why this might be true, we need to look at how the mind works.

You probably already know that the brain is hardwired to keep you safe from danger. ***Unfortunately, it cannot distinguish between imaginary fear and real dread.*** In other words, whether you are being chased by a large dog that just bit the postman or you're watching a zombie movie, the brain will get scared and cause anxiety, stress, and sometimes even persistent worry or panic.

At the end of the day, your ability to imagine fear often leads to real fear. But that's not the worst of it! ***Sometimes, the more scared you are, the scarier a situation appears.*** You might've gotten away from the dog, but for the rest of the way home, the fright you got makes all dogs you see appear more threatening.

## RAPID ODDITY

Scientists can identify emotions merely by looking at a person's **brain activity**.

## RAPID ODDITY

Your left cheek shows **more emotion** than your right cheek.

### PERSUASION AND EMOTIONS GO TOGETHER LIKE WATER AND OIL

One might think that emotions can easily sway people's opinions. After all, TV commercials play with your feelings all the time. ***However, researchers have discovered that using emotions to persuade others, especially in person, often backfires.*** This is unusual in itself because you're instinctively wired to use more emotional language to boost your powers of persuasion. As it turns out, the wiring doesn't go both ways, so you're not naturally receptive to such appeals! Indeed, most people quickly grasp when emotions are being used to influence them—and they don't like it.

**PSYCH TEST** A Friend Tractor Beam

Name the positive emotion that can draw new friends into your life!

a. Gratitude.
b. Happiness.
c. Kindness.
d. Humor.

## RAPID ODDITY

Can't pee with others nearby? This social anxiety is called "**paruresis**."

## WHEN OTHERS JUST DON'T GET YOU

Frustration comes in many flavors. But one of them is particularly, well, frustrating! This is when people don't get you. To clarify, it's not when you go emo and your parents fail to understand your new eyeliner and black wardrobe. ***This frustration, which is called "exulansis," happens when you talk to someone about an important experience but then realize that they cannot relate to or understand what you went through.*** Most people at the receiving end of exulansis become so exasperated that they abandon the conversation altogether.

## YOU MIGHT HAVE A NEUTRAL AFFECT

Affects can be described as a blend of your mood and emotions. Since humans are constantly fizzing with feelings, the popular view is that you cannot experience a moment of total neutrality. Supporters of this view believe that, even when you don't particularly think about anything, there's always an echo of emotion, like boredom or contentment.

However, some researchers believe that the neutral affect does exist. They compare it to indifference but it's not *the* indifference. Real indifference isn't neutral. ***There's always a smack of emotion that comes with it, and it's usually strongly negative*** (like avoidance or burnout).

But ironically, despite its name, total neutrality is not the hallmark of this affect. Contrary to what anti-neutral scientists believe, it's not the absence of all emotion but the presence of neutral feelings that creates this affect. ***You can experience neutrality while feeling low levels of negative or positive emotions.*** For example, while sitting at a restaurant, you're ready for dessert (low-level anticipation). You don't really have a preference (neutral affect) and flow with whatever the other guests are ordering.

## CAN YOU HEAR THE EMOTIONS?

When emotions are verbally expressed, the words themselves are not as important as the way in which they're being spoken. A child softly saying "Mommy" won't get the same response as when they scream the same word in terror. ***Researchers found that musicians, not moms, have a biological advantage in this case.*** Something about their training enables them to pick up on emotional cues in language better than others. Indeed, when they hear such a cue, their brain stems light up in a way that nonmusicians do not experience.

RAPID ODDITY

Happiness comes from not trying. Feeling pressured to be happy makes people **more depressed**.

## YOUR HANDS DETERMINE HOW YOUR BRAIN ORGANIZES EMOTIONS

At the core of your emotions sits motivation. In psychology, it is described as the drive to approach or withdraw from stimuli. For years, researchers thought that "approach motivation" happened in the left hemisphere of the brain, while the right side controlled "withdrawal motivation." However, a study by psychologists Geoffrey Brookshire and Daniel Casasanto finally revealed the fascinating truth: ***This process only counts for right-handed people. Left-handers experience this process in reverse.*** Their left lobe handles withdrawal motivation, and the right deals with approach.

**PSYCH TEST** **This Light Amps Up Your Emotions!**

Which type of light can amplify your mood, regardless of whether you are feeling positive or negative?

a. Blue light.
b. Low light.
c. Bright light.
d. Flickering lights.

## DROWN REGRET WITH COLD DRINKS

Ah, regret. That inner pit of fire where you roast yourself for doing something wrong. Remorse ranks high on the list of uncomfortable emotions, and it's a tough feeling to shake. But thanks to Western University in Canada, there might be a hack available the next time you find yourself in the pit. ***According to this study, a cold drink can quench the flames of regret.*** Researchers tested several groups of regretful volunteers and found that a chilled beverage or cool environment reduced their feelings of shame, embarrassment, and guilt.

One theory suggests that people instinctively perceive regret as "hot." Probably because blushing and other remorse-related feelings can literally flush your body with warmth. Nursing a cold drink can, apparently, soothe the hotness associated with regret.

Interestingly, this is not the first time that temperature has been linked with emotions. An earlier study found that holding a warm mug of coffee makes people more open to strangers, even viewing them as more trustworthy or friendly than they really are. On the other hand, a cold drink makes people more cautious of strangers.

**PSYCH TEST** Follow the Voice

Listening to your own speaking voice has an interesting effect on your mood. Pick the correct reason why this is.

- **a.** Being aware of your own voice is irritating.
- **b.** It can be distracting.
- **c.** You adjust your mood to match the emotions in your voice.
- **d.** It can make you feel self-important and confident.

## INTERESTED IN SOMETHING DULL? TIME TO SNOOZE

Not getting enough shut-eye can invite a host of crappy symptoms. ***But one of the weirdest ailments is how everything suddenly seems important.*** The strangeness begins when sleep deprivation seeps into the brain's emotional centers and upends their normal responses. According to researchers from Tel Aviv University, this makes you super-emotional. They discovered this, and more, when they kept volunteers awake all night and put these bleary-eyed people through several tests. The results showed that their brains eventually lost all neutrality and responded with gusto to dull and emotional images alike.

## RAPID ODDITY

Reading in one's native tongue **creates empathy**, but reading in a second language blunts emotions.

## RAPID ODDITY

**Sarcasm** is often used to hide feelings of vulnerability, anger, hostility, hurt, and fear.

**PSYCH TEST** This Emotion Is a Long-Distance Runner

Look at the emotions listed here. Which one, when compared to the others, stays with you the longest?

a. Surprise.
b. Fear.
c. Sadness.
d. Boredom.

### HERE'S WHY YOUR MOOD IS NOT AN EMOTION

***Emotions and mood are like fraternal twins—closely related but not identical.*** So what makes them different? Well, three things set them apart. First, emotions normally last a few minutes, whereas a mood can hang around for hours or days. Moods are also not a reaction, and emotions are provoked by a specific situation or person. Finally, emotions feel stronger. Think about rage or exhilaration! In contrast, moods are less intense. Indeed, you might not even be aware of what you're feeling until you consciously reflect upon your mood.

## RAPID ODDITY

Despite their fading memories, patients with Alzheimer's disease still experience **strong emotions**.

**PSYCH TEST** **Are You Guilty of Guilt?**

Choose the average number of hours that people spend feeling guilty about something every week.

a. One.
b. Three.
c. Five.
d. Eight.

## BOREDOM HAS A FREAKY EFFECT ON YOU

Boredom researchers are fascinated by the nature of this emotion and why people become bored—or, more importantly, what happens when you become bored. One particular experiment, designed by psychologists at the University of Florida, wanted to see just how far people would go to avoid boredom. So, they introduced volunteers to a lonely room and an electrocution device. *Gulp.*

Before the experiment began, the participants were allowed to test the machine, and everyone agreed that they did not enjoy the feeling of the shocks. The researchers then asked them to sit alone in the room where the device was their only "activity." The goal was to see if people would prefer pain over boredom, so the volunteers were allowed to shock themselves as they wished. And boy, did they.

***Roughly 25 percent of the women and 67 percent of the men chose to shock themselves rather than sit with their own thoughts.*** And not just one or two zings, either. People zapped themselves multiple times. One man had to be removed from the study because he totally overdid it.

## WHICH SCHADENFREUDE IS YOUR POISON?

"Schadenfreude" is a German word that roughly translates as "to feel joyful when something is damaged." ***In psychology, this term refers to the smug feeling you get when someone suffers a misfortune.*** Researchers now argue that this joy comes in three flavors, and they are all motivated by different emotions.

To illustrate, let's pretend that you are a soccer player. Your team loses by a massive margin, utterly crushed by the competition. The winning team's fans revel in your humiliation. This type of schadenfreude is motivated by an "us" versus "them" aggression. It occurs at sports events, between rival companies, and even between countries.

Feeling vengeful, you leave the stadium and deflate the tires of a car bearing the winning team's colors. The mean joy flowering in your heart is a second brand of schadenfreude motivated by spite and envy.

The third flavor is justice-motivated. A TV crew starts filming as you and the car's owner swat at each other before getting arrested by cops. The viewers enjoy this because they feel that a couple of hooligans got their just deserts.

### PSYCH TEST An Emotional Potion for Wisdom

Wisdom is a blend of good judgment and actions. But which emotional factors can also make you wiser?

a. Emotional control, empathy, and curiosity.
b. Inner peace and charity.
c. Happiness, poise, and helpfulness.
d. Cheerfulness, compassion, and love.

## RAPID ODDITY

"Macro grief" describes the **collective sorrow** felt by millions when a war or pandemic strikes.

## DEALING WITH REMORSE—THE ELVISH WAY

Harry Potter fans are familiar with a character called Dobby. This house elf had the habit of punishing himself whenever he felt guilty about a mistake, usually by banging his head against something. ***This tendency to punish oneself to show remorse has been dubbed the "Dobby effect."*** Psychologists believe that some people subconsciously seek out pain to relieve unresolved guilt. Others use it as a dramatic signal to apologize to whomever they hurt, especially when they know that a benevolent gesture, like giving flowers, won't patch up their mistake.

### PSYCH TEST Employees Gone Wild

When employees are monitored with surveillance, what negative effect can this have on their emotions and actions?

a. More rule-breaking and resentment.
b. Depression and slower work.
c. Anger and more resignations.
d. Making more mistakes due to stress.

## RAPID ODDITY

Guilt can make you feel **physically heavier and bigger** than you really are.

**PSYCH TEST** **The Wonder of Awe**

Amazing experiences often trigger a sense of wonder. Name the emotional benefits that come with awe.

a. It makes you laugh more.
b. It calms and refreshes the mind.
c. Your ability to learn new information deepens.
d. You maintain a happy mood for longer.

## 3D MOVIE EMOTIONS FALL FLAT OF THE HYPE

With the advent of three-dimensional films came the belief that these realistic movies provoke more emotion than 2D. Psychologists in Utah wanted to see if this was indeed the case. They strapped over four hundred volunteers into gadgets designed to measure their emotional responses. While they watched movies in 2D or 3D, these devices recorded their breathing, heart rate, cardiovascular responses, and sweaty palms. These are all trustworthy emotional thermometers, and they quickly provided the study with an answer. ***Both types of films are very adept at creating emotion, but neither is better than the other.***

## RAPID ODDITY

**Coziness** gives you emotional benefits such as reduced anxiety, more optimism, and positivity.

# CHAPTER 6

# FORENSIC PSYCHOLOGY AND ABNORMAL PSYCHOLOGY: THE PSYCHOLOGY OF THE CRIMINAL

Did you know that psychology has a dark side? Dark psychology is all about how psychological principles can be used to control and even harm other people. Most people fall prey to the effects of dark psychology without even realizing it, like guilt trips, pickup artists, and other forms of manipulation. But that's only scraping the surface....The trivia facts in this chapter also explore negative emotions, the fields of forensic and abnormal psychology, and the darkest of personalities.

The good news is that this chapter has a double purpose: Not only will you be at the top of your psychology trivia game; you'll also be primed to spot some of these psychological tricks at work! In this chapter, you'll dive headfirst into the dark side of psychology and cover topics like the most dangerous personality trait (no, it's not psychopathy), why staring at someone's forehead will actually make them nervous, and where a curious process called "fear then relief" is common in everyday life. You can look forward to learning more about a perky condition called "reverse paranoia," how pollen fights crime, and when empaths (who are the sweethearts on the personality spectrum) can turn into utter creeps!

Be warned: These trivia facts are not for the faint of heart!

## RAPID ODDITY

Some experts estimate that **one in every two hundred** Americans has narcissistic personality disorder.

### FREUD GAVE NARCISSISM A THUMBS-UP

Nobody in their right mind can give narcissism a silver lining...right? The founding father of psychoanalysis did exactly that. ***Sigmund Freud considered the self-absorption and lack of empathy that he noticed in young children to be normal.*** However, even though he was fine with the atomic tantrums of toddlers, Freud had his limits. He argued that narcissism is a big problem should it persist after puberty.

**PSYCH TEST** This Silver Lining Has a Dark Cloud

Which negative trait is common among people who have empathy for others?

- **a.** Procrastination.
- **b.** A deep sense of guilt.
- **c.** Secretly judging others.
- **d.** Low self-esteem.

## RAPID ODDITY

People with "dark triad" personality traits (narcissism, Machiavellianism, and psychopathy) are more likely to **ghost their dating partners**.

## HOW TO LOOK DODGY DURING A CONVERSATION

There are many reasons why someone might hesitate before answering a question. Some need a moment to process the question and their own response. Or maybe they just ate a cookie and don't want to reply with their mouth full. Unfortunately, even the most honest pause can make others doubt your sincerity when you finally talk. ***Studies have shown that a slow response is often viewed as stalling, either to avoid the truth or to tell a lie.*** On the flip side, a speedy denial to the question "Have you seen my cookies?" might get you off the hook.

### PSYCH TEST A Simple Skill That Foils Psychopaths

Psychopaths, especially those who commit violent crimes, often are unable to perform which essential social skill?

a. Recognize facial expressions.
b. Respond to different tones of voice.
c. Resolve conflict with others.
d. Make eye contact.

## EVEN EXPERTS BORROW SORROW

***Despite their training to deal with emotions, psychologists are not immune to trauma.*** They're particularly vulnerable to vicarious trauma. This happens when a psychologist absorbs a terrible event by listening to someone. For example, a victim might recount a terrible ordeal, or, during an interview with a killer, the tragic details of the crime become too much. The symptoms are nasty. Psychologists can develop a preoccupation with the case or become numb to it. Insomnia, nightmares, eating disorders, anger, reduced life or work satisfaction, and feelings of guilt are also common.

## REVERSE PARANOIA—OPTIMISM ON STEROIDS

Paranoia is a deep suspicion of unseen threats and doubting other people's motives, especially when there's no evidence to support these feelings. While most are familiar with this term, few people are aware of the disorder's strange twin. This perky condition is called "reverse paranoia," or "pronoia."

***Pronoia is the persistent belief that everyone—even the universe—is plotting to do good in your life.*** In some instances, the delusion is not harmful at all. But imagine the consequences of putting your faith in dangerous criminals or investing a lot of money in a sinking asset, purely based on the notion that all people and opportunities are there to help you.

Some experts view pronoia as an extreme form of denial or a coping mechanism that relies on toxic positivity to get by. But the darkest form of this condition has nothing to do with the avoidance of pain. Whereas some cases just look at the world through rose-tinted glasses, others are downright narcissistic. They expect special treatment because they're "better" than others.

## ABNORMAL PSYCHOLOGY IS THE ODD KID OUT

This branch of psychology is often at the center of much debate. What *is* "normal," and, more importantly, who gets to *decide* what's "normal"? Indeed, what is normal in one culture might be weird for another; there are too many factors involved to satisfy everybody's definition of the word. ***Instead, psychologists in this field often look at how much distress a behavior causes someone or how badly it disrupts their life.*** When a certain behavior or thought pattern has negative consequences, it's considered "abnormal" for that individual.

**PSYCH TEST Sometimes It's Best to Not Think**

In abnormal psychology, experts have identified about twenty thought disorders. Which main characteristic do they all share?

a. Struggling to communicate coherent thoughts and speech.
b. The inability to form normal memories.
c. Vivid hallucinations and delusions.
d. Getting trapped in thoughts and memories.

## YOU'RE A SERIAL KILLER? LET'S GET MARRIED!

***Hybristophilia is the abnormal desire to be the love interest of a convicted, brutal criminal.*** This phenomenon is why violent killers like Ted Bundy and Richard Ramirez had courtroom groupies, and why convicted wife-killer Scott Peterson received a marriage proposal while on death row.

Human behavior is notoriously wonky, but why would anyone crave romantic involvement with someone who murdered their previous love interest, as with the Peterson case? While forensic psychologists encounter this a lot in their field, the topic is not well studied. A definite explanation for what seems like a fatal attraction is not yet on the cards.

One theory suggests that it's not really about the thrill of the threat. Instead, these people might like the limelight, whether it's a news crew filming them or seeing their families shocked. The theory doesn't end there, and here's where things get less magical for the incarcerated partner: ***Those with hybristophilia could prefer a partner behind bars because a free-range love interest might not need them as much.*** Those with hybristophilia also know where their boo is at all times and don't have to worry about picking up their socks or finding traces of an affair.

## RAPID ODDITY

A survey by Southern Methodist University of 1.6 million Americans found that Washington, DC, has the **highest concentration** of psychopaths.

## A MYSTERIOUS PSYCHOSIS HAMPERS NEW MOMS

Some women experience the "baby blues," a form of depression brought on by post-birth hormonal processes. This is very normal, and the condition, which is characterized by mild mood changes, usually resolves itself.

***Unfortunately, one in five hundred new mothers will experience psychosis instead.*** Symptoms can appear quickly, sometimes within hours of the birth, or weeks later. These include hallucinations, delusions, mania, loss of inhibitions, a total change in character, confusion, and paranoia.

Women with the baby blues need a healthy and understanding environment. But this is not the remedy for postpartum psychosis. Experts consider the condition a medical emergency that is threatening to both the mother and the baby. Treatment requires hospitalization and antipsychotic medication, as well as mood stabilizers.

***Birth psychosis is a mysterious condition without any known cause.*** Those who appear to be more at risk include people with schizophrenia or bipolar disorder and a family history of mental illness. Mothers who were previously successfully treated for postpartum psychosis are also more likely to experience it again.

## RAPID ODDITY

Due to their ruthlessness and charisma, narcissists are more likely to be **promoted to CEOs**.

## POLLEN POLICES THE STREETS...?

Something is pacifying offenders, and it seems to be floating around in the air. True enough, when researchers, published in the *Journal of Health Economics*, did a deep dive into the statistics of violent crimes across sixteen US cities, ***they noticed a steep decline during the pollen season***. It's not clear how these tiny poofs can stop an assault before it even happens. But in all likelihood, the unwell feelings that come with hay fever, such as headaches and stuffed sinuses, might dampen a person's enthusiasm to go out and hold up a liquor store.

## THE DARK TRIAD'S CREEPY FRIEND

The dark triad is bad news. There's psychopathy, hiding its remorseless nature behind a charming smile. Machiavellianism is a power freak that will crush any moral standard to manipulate others. Then there's narcissism, with its entitlement and grandiose ideas.

Researchers suspect that this group might not be complete. There's a fourth candidate, and, cruelty-wise, it could be the worst of them all. ***This shadowy character is sadism.***

Since sadists cannot commit crimes in a laboratory, scientists found another way to test cruelty: they gave pill bugs cute names. For most people, a pill bug named Tootsie is more humanized and thus harder to kill. The sadistic volunteers had no such qualms. They happily put Tootsie through a loud grinder (unbeknownst to them, the machine was safe for the animal).

The apparent pill bug massacre was a "reward" for something else, but a second test revealed the true terror of sadism. This time there was no reward. But the sadists knuckled down and even weathered obstacles to mete out cruelty to what they believed were real human opponents in a computer game. ***None of the other dark triad personalities inflict suffering without gain, only sadism.***

## RAPID ODDITY

Research indicates that narcissists have a **flawed brain**, which prevents them from feeling empathy.

**PSYCH TEST** **Some Empaths Are Creepy Too**

Empaths are people who can internalize and sympathize with others' feelings, making them great friends and caregivers. But which trait makes you a dark empath?

a. A distinct desire to hurt other people's feelings.
b. The ability to recognize and manipulate someone's emotions.
c. Faking empathy for personal gain.
d. Denying the importance of someone's feelings.

## BEWARE THAT RELIEF!

Meet FTR, the glitch that makes you more cooperative. This "fear then relief" reaction is used by salespeople, manipulative partners, and interrogators to influence others. ***They cause, then abruptly remove, a source of anxiety, knowing that the relief might make you more open to requests.*** For example, a salesperson spews hairy crime statistics until you're convinced that a burglar's going to crawl across your lawn *tonight*. After shredding your sense of safety, the salesperson suddenly provides a "solution." In this case, the security products they're selling. Psychologists believe that people with a high need for closure are more susceptible to such scare tactics because accepting the solution helps them to cope with the confusion of the sudden change.

## PANIC ATTACKS CAN POUNCE WHILE YOU'RE SLEEPING

The panic attacks that most people are familiar with happen during the day. When one occurs, it tends to ruin the next twenty minutes with symptoms like sweaty palms, jelly legs, a racing heart, and a feeling of intense fear. The intensity level can range from bad anxiety to literally thinking you are about to die. ***But this panic disorder can also invade sleep.***

As bizarre as that sounds, a sufferer could be snoring and dreaming about something pleasant when, out of the blue, they are yanked awake by a panic attack. The symptoms are similar to a daytime episode, but the night terror can also cause sweating all over the body, mental disorientation, and even a fear of going back to sleep.

But what causes nocturnal panic attacks? Nobody knows. ***Some experts suggest that they have mixed roots in stressful times, genetics, and hormonal changes.*** The condition can also be brought on by other anxiety disorders such as PTSD and obsessive-compulsive tendencies. But at the end of the day (or night), one can at least take comfort in the fact that panic attacks are not dangerous.

## WHY ARE YOU STARING AT MY...FOREHEAD?

Body language plays a major role in communication. Your mind is primed to detect such signals—especially during conversations. Let's say that you're talking to someone. Where this person's eyes land on your face can betray their feelings about you. Are you conversing with a lip-gazer? You're likely attractive to them. Are they refusing to break eye contact? They're probably trying to dominate you. But a person who stares at your forehead is just awkward. Sensing a negative vibe? Well done. ***Body language experts say that brow-watchers don't care for you or don't care for what you're saying.***

**PSYCH TEST** **Why Depression Erases Colors**

People with depression claim to see less color. In some cases, this is true, but what is the scientific explanation behind this unusual symptom?

a. Depression slows retinal response to color contrasts.
b. The brain lacks focus.
c. Chemicals related to depression interfere with color perception.
d. It's an illusion caused by feeling uninterested in the world around you.

## HOW TO SPOT A SOCIOPATH VERSUS A PSYCHOPATH

Let's say a neighbor behaves in a way that might concern the FBI. The family across the street calls him a sociopath, but the person next door is convinced he's a psychopath. Both labels are often loosely given to anyone with mean, antisocial behavior, but they're not the same. ***Psychologists have identified two major differences.*** Psychopaths have no remorse. Sociopaths can have a weak conscience. A psychopath's violence is also more methodical and planned. A sociopath tends to be a hot mess and reacts impulsively when angry or confronted.

### RAPID ODDITY

According to the Centre for Addiction and Mental Health, about 3 percent of all people will experience a **psychotic episode** in their life.

## RAPID ODDITY

Your mind sees someone holding a gun as **bigger and stronger** than they really are.

## BE NICE, PSYCHOPATHS HAVE FEELINGS TOO

Considering their scant regard for other people's feelings, ***it's hard to believe that psychopaths can also feel love, sadness, and loneliness—but it's true.*** Studies have even found that the death of a spouse can cause them grief. Some psychopaths also suffer emotionally because they're not happy with their own deviant behavior.

Researchers have also learned that, at their innermost core, individuals with this darkness want to be loved and cared for—just like everybody else. But their repellant qualities push people away and deprive them of this basic human need.

Although most psychopaths are aware that it's their own behavior causing suffering to others and themselves, they can only return affection on their own terms. This doesn't exactly make them more endearing.

Contrary to popular belief, having psychopathic traits doesn't automatically mean you want to hunt people with a spear. There are "successful" psychopaths who channel their personality into shark-tank professions like law and politics. They never commit a crime. ***But scientists suspect that those who reach a certain point of loneliness, low life satisfaction, or poor self-esteem can turn into a threat.***

## RAPID ODDITY

A workplace frenemy can do **more psychological damage** to their colleagues than an outright enemy.

## DON'T FOLLOW THE BREAD CRUMBS

In romantic relationships, it's always a good sign when you arrive home and there's a trail of rose petals inviting you deeper into the house. Unfortunately, some people get a trail of bread crumbs. This is not a good thing. ***In psychology, you've been "bread-crumbed" when somebody leads you on.***

While it can happen in other contexts, this behavior most commonly abuses romantic interests. The term basically means that you are being given crumbs of attention or affection—just enough to keep you invested in the other person. However, they never plan on giving you the full buffet.

Why do people crumb their suitors? In the majority of cases, it's about standing on a pedestal and being admired. In short, they keep their "love interest" hanging because they enjoy the ego boost when someone is enamored with them.

***Bread-crumbing also has the toxic ability to make victims yearn for a deeper connection with the object of their affection.*** This blinds them to what is going on, despite feeling hurt and confused. This need for acceptance is why some victims get dragged along the gravelly road of disappointment for months.

**PSYCH TEST** **Can You Do Me Another Favor?**

Which strategy do people use to make others comply to first small, then larger demands?

a. The foot-in-the-door technique.
b. The escalator method.
c. Four stages of compliance.
d. Blackmail.

**PSYCH TEST** **Watch Out for This Weather!**

Machiavellians are known for some pretty dark traits, like their cold, cynical, and manipulative nature. But in which weather conditions do they actually appear more appealing to others?

a. Complete darkness.
b. Cloudy weather.
c. Rainy weather.
d. A beautiful, sunny day.

## RAPID ODDITY

A victim is "hoovered" when a rejected, toxic individual **manipulates** them into resuming contact.

## IF THE DARK TRIAD WERE CLOWNS...

Humor is generally a positive thing. But how does it change shape when the dark personalities get their hands on it? ***Interestingly, studies have shown that each member of the dark triad leans toward a different style of humor even though they all use it to advance their own selfish goals.*** Machiavellians like to use irony to put others down. Narcissists prefer wit and other styles of lighter humor to cozy up to their victims. Psychopaths go straight for the jugular with sarcasm, cynicism, and mockery.

**PSYCH TEST** **911? Yeah, I'm Guilty...**

Many murderers call 911 as a "bystander" to report their crimes. During these calls, how do they often give themselves away?

a. They let slip that they're the killer.
b. Their story keeps changing.
c. Murderers are more theatrical and less forthright.
d. They don't sound shocked by the gruesome crime.

## JERKOLOGY 101

The study of jerks, or jerkology, is a thing. While it's not an official term, experts are looking into what makes somebody a jerk. Apparently, it's not that easy. There are no cut-and-dried traits like with the dark triad that can identify a jerk with 100 percent accuracy. ***Instead, it seems to be a gut feeling that most people have.*** They just know when they see a jerk. Researchers have also noticed that the ability to spot one makes people feel smug, as if seeing a jerk somehow proves that they themselves are not one.

**RAPID ODDITY**

Empathetic people are a **favorite prey** of narcissists because they tend to forgive bad behavior.

## NARCISSISTS CAN BE VULNERABLE TOO

Did scientists finally discover a narcissist with empathy? Regrettably not. However, they did identify a subspecies, so to speak, of the narcissists we all know and do not love. Whereas the usual lot displays tons of self-confidence and charisma and soaks up the attention of others, the so-called vulnerable narcissists do things differently.

They still think they are better than everybody else. They also lack empathy for anyone except themselves. ***But vulnerable narcissists are overly sensitive in the sense that they cannot handle criticism.*** Indeed, any scrutiny might feel like a personal attack on them. Even if you give a vulnerable narcissist a compliment (which a normal narcissist would love), they'll corrupt the moment. For example, they'll mistrust the reason why you complimented them and also wonder how you are trying to attack them with it.

Needless to say, this can be emotionally draining for romantic partners, family, and even coworkers of such an individual. Mistrust is not the only problem. ***They also tend to be so secretive and detached from those around them that loved ones often feel defeated, angry, and invisible.***

## A MURDERER'S AURA FOR SALE

A lot of people collect things. But one group gravitates toward hoarding murder memorabilia. Such items could be the killer's socks or a bloodied pebble found at a crime scene. Naturally, people are wondering why. What appeal draws collectors to have a passion for something connected to a brutal death? According to researchers, there is an interesting psychological effect at play—and a rather dark one. ***Collectors of murderabilia are vitalized by the dangerous "aura" of these objects***, often because they are attracted to the extreme way that the killer smashed society's rules.

## RAPID ODDITY

Contrary to popular belief, people with mental illness are **more likely to be victims** than perpetrators.

## CONFESSIONS OF A BURGLAR

To gain more information about how burglaries work and to provide the public with information they can use to secure their homes better, researchers from the University of North Carolina went straight to the problem. They asked over four hundred burglars what motivated them to crawl through people's windows and what made them think twice and leave empty-handed. ***The survey showed that the main motivation for burglary was money and drugs***, not the theft of weapons, as commonly believed. And although the following isn't a foolproof way to safeguard one's castle, most burglars said that they would avoid a house with alarms, dogs, and nearby traffic.

**PSYCH TEST** Why Are You So Quiet?

Introvert-shaming is a destructive trend perpetuated by more outgoing personalities. What is the main sign of this shaming?

a. Spreading false rumors about someone.
b. Mocking or bullying an individual for staying in the background.
c. Forcing introverts into socially draining situations.
d. Publicly laughing at introverts.

**PSYCH TEST When Older Siblings Sin**

When an older brother or sister commits a violent crime, what influence can this have on their younger siblings?

a. Depression in later life.
b. Post-traumatic stress disorder and a sense of betrayal.
c. Poor academic performance.
d. A greater risk of following in their footsteps.

## WHEN YOUR THERAPY CLIENT IS BATMAN

When it comes to fictional crime fighters, none quite compare to Batman. He's mysterious, a parkour master (it seems), and he knows how to punch jokers. And that poker face! The latter came under scrutiny recently when psychologists led by Travis Langley decided to analyze Batman as if he were a real person—just to see what he was thinking and to assess his mental health.

***The analysis showed that Bruce Wayne could possibly have five mental disorders.*** He witnessed his parents' murder as a child, and his behavior strongly suggests that Batman has post-traumatic stress disorder (PTSD). The deep guilt over his parents and the death of Robin might also have given him depression.

His obsession with criminals controls his life, suggesting obsessive-compulsive disorder. The fact that he sometimes refers to himself in the third person while in costume also hints at multiple personality disorder. Finally, his scant regard for the law and bystanders (at times) doesn't make him psychotic, but researchers suspect a related disorder: antisocial personality disorder (characterized by a lack of both conscience and respect for other people's feelings, rights, and needs).

## RAPID ODDITY

According to the **broken windows theory**, areas with vandalized buildings invite more criminal activity.

**PSYCH TEST** Punishing a Psychopath Is...Complicated

To deter re-offending, punishment follows a convicted crime. Why doesn't this work for psychopaths?

a. They love violence too much.
b. Their brains do not understand punishment.
c. Incarceration teaches them to be more violent.
d. They tend to become institutionalized, not rehabilitated.

### HEROES MIGHT NOT BE SO BENEVOLENT

Most people view heroes and psychopaths as polar opposites. ***But when researchers compared their traits, they found that both types share a high degree of fearlessness.*** This trait is considered a basis for psychopathy. The idea that heroes might be a brand of psychopath harks back to the 1980s, but the theory is controversial. Some experts suggest that heroes are noncriminal and socialized psychopaths, while the violent type suffers from pathological psychopathy. They even suggest that if heroes had different childhood experiences, they might've committed crimes instead of heroic acts.

## RAPID ODDITY

People are more put off by **humblebragging** than straightforward bragging.

**PSYCH TEST Only the Narcissist Can Shine**

Which tactic do narcissists commonly use when someone's achievements take the spotlight away from them?

a. Minimizing the achievements.
b. Spreading lies about the person or situation.
c. Pretending they also achieved the same thing.
d. It often triggers an angry outburst.

## ALL VIOLENT CRIMINALS ARE PSYCHOPATHS, RIGHT? NOT QUITE...

When heinous acts are committed, it's easy to lump all violent criminals together as psychopaths. But according to the experts, ***distinct traits separate a true psychopathic offender from your regular bloodthirsty criminal***. The latter tends to be hyperresponsive when cornered, threatened, or insulted. They also display clear aggression and have short fuses. Meanwhile, most psychopaths keep their cool during a threatening situation, like arrest, and their tempers are rarely quick. Another major difference is that psychopaths also lean toward premeditated crimes and well-planned acts of aggression.

### RAPID ODDITY

Using **agreeable euphemisms** for repulsive things is a powerful way to sway a reluctant public.

## THE SHELL GAME—NOT AS CUTE AS IT SOUNDS

The "shell game" is a manipulative technique toxic people use—notably, abusive partners and political leaders. This method is incredibly well woven and can drive a normal person to the end of their rope.

Those who play the shell game rely on four traits: being all-knowing, all-good, all-powerful, and never self-contradictory. Try reasoning with someone like that! ***They play the game by shifting between the traits as they need them or using one trait to deny another.*** That's why it's called the "shell game." When you call them out on one, they slip into another like it's a protective shell. It sounds simple, but it can be impossible to deal with.

Shelling isn't just used by people who are easy-to-spot jerks. Sometimes, toxic "victims" can also manipulate people and circumstances by playing up the all-good factor, going full martyr when confronted for doing something wrong. ***These individuals also use goodness as a weapon.*** For example, one minute they are a saint who can do no evil (all-good), and the next, they use their godlike righteousness (all-power) to justify hurting others.

## HOW TO FREAK OUT A NARCISSIST

Narcissists are experts at being "invincible" and "amazing." They can fake a glamorous lifestyle, smoothly convince people that they're a brain surgeon or astronaut, and appear generally fearless. However, there is a chink in their armor: ***They dread certain feelings, and most narcissists will go to great lengths to avoid them.*** Someone with a healthy mindset also does not like to be humiliated or to land in a situation that leaves them feeling inferior. But whereas most people can work through such an unfortunate day, narcissists fear these vulnerable feelings down to their bones.

**PSYCH TEST** **Negative Brownie Points**

Brownie points are an imaginary social currency that is earned by doing good deeds. How do manipulators use it to get their own way?

a. They only favor people who do things for them.
b. After doing someone a favor, they milk it for months.
c. They brag about their good deeds to gain more favor.
d. They break down others' good behavior to steal the show.

## TROLLS ARE A HAPPY LOT

***Researchers from The Australian Institute found that one in three Internet users has been the victim of online abuse.*** If you do the math, that's countless cases of harassment. This piqued the interest of scientists, who were concerned about the seemingly endless army of Internet trolls and their ability to destroy someone's life.

The study wanted to understand the psychological reason why these people make others so miserable. A leading theory suggested that these shadowy figures ruin other people's day (or reputation) because they themselves suffer from low self-worth.

On the surface, this assumption made sense. Many abusers, and narcissists in particular, kick people down a notch so that they can feel "above" their victims. It's a cheap tactic, but it works. However, when the researchers surveyed online users to find these abusers, another picture emerged—one that was more sinister than low self-esteem.

On average, most Internet trolls have psychopathic and sadistic traits. They also have high self-esteem, so they don't view their own behavior as a call for help. On the contrary, ***when they actively provoke and harm others, they feel pretty good about themselves***.

**PSYCH TEST I'm Ignoring You**

When someone gives them the silent treatment, people often assume that they're just fuming. Why is this behavior actually sinister?

a. It breaks down healthy communication.
b. People become angrier with each other.
c. It punishes, hurts, and manipulates a partner.
d. This behavior is a good indicator of a future divorce.

## MEET GASLIGHTING'S COUSIN: MOONWALKING

People associate a lot of good things with moonwalking. There was the historical moment when Neil Armstrong's toes became the first human contact with the moon. But then there's the psychological abuse technique called "moonwalking." ***Similar to gaslighting, its ultimate goal is to wear a victim down.*** But where gaslighting makes you question your mind and reality, moonwalking is basically a trap. The abuser purposefully steps on a nerve just to get an angry or upset reaction—and then guilt-trips and belittles the victim for "overreacting."

**RAPID ODDITY**

When a victim of gaslighting believes an abuser's lies, they often start to **gaslight themselves**.

## RAPID ODDITY

Narcissists **project their mistakes** onto others; a cheater might accuse their innocent partner of infidelity.

## GRIEVING? IT'S SHOWTIME FOR THESE GUYS

One of the most ridiculous things that narcissists love to steal from other people is their right to mourn. ***The narcissist wants to be the center of activity—even when it's a funeral.*** For example, when their spouse loses a parent, the spouse can expect little support. The narcissist will keep telling the guests how the death affected them and not their partner. They'll even sob on their spouse's shoulder to show how much the whole thing devastated them.

### PSYCH TEST Doing Business with the Dark Triad? Try This!

Smooth-talking, calculating dark triad personalities (narcissists, Machiavellians, and psychopaths) have an unfair advantage in business deals. Which simple tactic removes it?

a. Communicate with them online.
b. Double-check all their "kind" offers for pitfalls.
c. Educate your team about the triad's manipulation tactics.
d. Avoid such business partners as much as possible.

**PSYCH TEST** **Two Jerks in a Room...**

For negotiations, a popular choice is to use a well-liked and diplomatic person. What might happen if two disagreeable individuals talked instead?

a. Total chaos.
b. A high chance of a successful meeting.
c. A low chance of a mutually beneficial deal.
d. Lasting enmity between the two businesses.

## THE DARK SIDE OF DAYLIGHT SAVING TIME

When daylight saving time ends and clocks turn back an hour, most people look forward to some extra sleep. A well-rested society is more peaceful, right? Nope. When research published in the *Journal of Experimental Criminology* looked at the crime statistics on the Monday following the end of daytime saving time, they found that assaults spiked on that day. The opposite was true when daylight saving time began; on the Monday following, assaults dropped. ***As it turns out, getting more sleep just refreshes the angry birds.*** Getting less sleep might make some people more irritable, but they're too lethargic to tackle others.

## RAPID ODDITY

Everyone has **self-soothing prejudice**, the tendency to look for flaws in someone who seems better than them!

## THINK LIKE A BURGLAR

Researchers from the United Kingdom and Spain joined forces to investigate how logic and decision-making played a role in burglaries. For this, they needed to talk to three groups: ordinary citizens, the burglars that rob them, and the police who chase those running away with a stolen TV.

For this study, 120 volunteers were questioned. Divided into three groups of forty, the ordinary people, criminals, and cops, all had to give their opinion on one thing. After they were given several factors related to security and different scenarios, they had to study and use them to predict the odds of a home being burgled.

Interestingly, all three groups had different leanings. The closest any of them came to agreeing was when the police officers and citizens considered that the most relevant factor was the method burglars chose to break in. However, the homeowners were less consistent with the rest of their survey answers than the cops, who seemed to think alike. ***The burglars, on the other hand, were most concerned about the presence of a house alarm and not their method.***

### PSYCH TEST A Leafy Influence on Lawbreakers

Trees in cities add beauty and shade to the streets. But what effect do urban trees have on crime?

a. More hiding places for criminals.
b. Reduced property damage and violent crimes.
c. A calming effect on angry (and potentially violent) minds.
d. More trees often lead to more thefts and vandalism.

## RAPID ODDITY

**The perks of having narcissism include lower stress levels and a reduced risk of depression.**

### WHEN MEDITATION ISN'T SO ZEN

The ancient art of meditation is arguably one of the best things that humanity has ever invented. Just consider the mental benefits. According to the Mayo Clinic, this inner stillness can bring more resilience, greater self-awareness, and relaxation. And that's just looking at the tip of this iceberg! Speaking of icebergs...some people get the RMS *Titanic* treatment.

***Indeed, for some, the psychological effects of meditation can swing the wrong way.*** Brown University uncovered this shady side when it interviewed almost one hundred people. The volunteers didn't just include students with different levels of experience but also meditation teachers who have been practicing for years.

The participants frequently reported side effects. Physically, they became oversensitive to sound and light and suffered from insomnia and involuntary body movements. But emotionally, things were perhaps more draining. Practitioners ran the full gamut of nervous reactions, from anxiety and fear to intense feelings of panic.

The study also found that some sought-after experiences—like feeling a complete oneness with others—totally disturbed some people, who felt violated and even disorientated when the feeling wouldn't go away.

## GIVE THESE GUYS A MINUTE

***Since stun guns have joined the force, the US police have tasered over two million citizens.*** Scientists were concerned about the cognitive consequences of taking a 50,000-volt shock, since suspects have to be fully aware of their rights at the point of arrest. To get a few frazzled brains to study, Drexel University and Arizona State University tased over seventy volunteers. Frighteningly, while some showed low brain impairment, others had learning impairments comparable to those experienced by people with Alzheimer's disease. ***This suggests that stunned suspects probably need a breather before they can listen to their Miranda warning.***

### PSYCH TEST How to Spot a Fugitive 101

For the moment, let's ignore the stereotypes found in movie fugitives. What behavior points to a *real* fugitive?

a. Bragging about something they've done.
b. Real fugitives are exceptionally boring people.
c. A sudden violent act.
d. Lying about their past.

## RAPID ODDITY

Most offenders have a unique "**territory**," an area they stick to when committing crimes.

The number one food item stolen from supermarkets is **cheese**.

## THE STRANGE LONG-TERM DREAMS OF PSYCHOPATHS

What happens when a psychopath scribbles in their goal-planning notebook? Researchers found such individuals are very goal-driven and that they plan well in the short term. They also tend to excel when they wing their plans for the day. But when they set their sights on the distant future, that's when things become distorted. ***This group is often unable to anchor their dreams in reality.*** For example, when several psychopaths were interviewed in prison—emphasis on the fact that they're incarcerated—some said that they wanted to join law enforcement agencies like the FBI.

### PSYCH TEST Too Much of a Bad Thing

Deviant behavior is influenced by many things. But the exposure to which unfortunate factor during childhood can lead to aggressive criminal behavior in adulthood?

- **a.** Signs of gang activity in one's neighborhood.
- **b.** Domestic violence.
- **c.** Too much lead in the environment.
- **d.** Drug use.

## YOU'RE A DANGER TO SOCIETY? YOU'RE HIRED!

Few people think about this, but dangerous people, like serial killers, also need to pay the bills. Naturally, this got researchers thinking: Do violent offenders take any job that comes their way, or do they have a preference?

When researchers compiled a list of where criminals go when it's time to do some honest slogging, there were a few surprises. ***For some reason, serial killers gravitated toward certain careers, but not always the ones that fed their dark side.*** None worked at slaughterhouses or cemeteries.

The study divided convicted killers according to their education levels and then considered the top occupations of each group. Skilled serial killers tended to be aircraft machinists, shoemakers, repair people, and—wait for this one—that guy who installs upholstery in cars. Semiskilled murderers dwelled in greenery as forest workers or arborists, managed warehouses, and drove trucks. Unskilled offenders were general laborers, hotel porters, and gas station attendants.

Perhaps the most frightening serial killers were the ones with professional or government-related jobs. Their top career preferences included police officers, security officials, military personnel, and religious officials.

### RAPID ODDITY

Inmates who don't experience two things, **remorse and accepting responsibility**, are likelier to re-offend.

## OFFICE WORKERS: THE WORLD'S BIGGEST THIEVES!

Forget bank heists! ***When it comes to lucrative thefts, nobody beats the people who work in retail.*** When they illegally fill their pockets, the most popular loot includes writing stationery, sticky notes, paper clips, and the occasional chair. This adds up to $40 billion in losses every year. But what motivates someone to walk away with a paper clip? According to one report, employees have different reasons, like anger toward an employer, feeling entitled to take something, and the belief that stealing a cheap pencil won't hurt the company.

**PSYCH TEST** **You Can Blame the Parents for This One**

Which important life decision made by parents can steer their adolescent child toward crime?

a. Giving their child an unpopular name.
b. Forcing a teenager to work in the family business.
c. Deciding not to finance their child's dreams and goals.
d. Getting a divorce.

## THE STRANGE LETHARGY OF A CRIMINAL'S FAMILY

In most cases, people will react with disgust or condemnation when they hear about a serious crime—***unless the groper, stalker, or blackmailer is their own family member***. Indeed, the very same people who might report an offender to the police—if the person is a stranger—will often do nothing when they learn that the home invader that's been terrorizing the neighborhood is, in fact, one of their own. Psychologists believe that this double standard hinges on misplaced loyalty, love, and even the desire not to stigmatize the family's reputation.

**PSYCH TEST** **Your Brain Is a Nighttime Nag**

More often than not, your brain fixates on negative thoughts when you go to bed. Pick the psychological reason why this happens.

a. The mind cannot shut off due to a busy day.
b. Obsessive-compulsive disorder.
c. It's a survival strategy.
d. The brain's fear center is most active just before sleep.

## WHEN TWO HEARTS BEAT FOR THEMSELVES

When narcissists date people who do not have malignant personality traits, the love inevitably turns into a toxic situation. Researchers were curious to know what might happen if two narcissists dated each other. Would they despise each other from the start? Surprisingly, their study published in *Personality and Individual Differences* showed that ***narcissists often prefer their own kind when it comes to a romantic partner***. Even though such a relationship might come with special challenges, it's a classic example of "assortative mating," or the desire to have a mate who is similar to oneself.

**RAPID ODDITY**

Psychopaths **can feel fear**, but they lack other people's automatic detection and reactivity to threats.

# CHAPTER 7

# SOCIAL PSYCHOLOGY: THE CROWD, CONSUMER, AND CULT MIND

Can't resist that Black Friday sale, can you? It's not your fault! Ever galloped toward a bargain or watched parents fight over the last Elmo doll in the store? Then this chapter is for you! Here, you will look at the amazing psychology of today's consumer culture—and it is more bizarre than you think.

While it's certainly entertaining to learn more about why people buy, the trivia in this chapter also serves a more important purpose. Retailers are wizards when it comes to wielding psychology—especially fears and biases—to make you spend more. Once you discover the most common and powerful marketing tricks, then you can protect your budget from buyer's remorse!

The branch of psychology that peeks into shoppers' carts is called "social psychology." This field also studies the crowd mind, and, for this reason, the following pages are full of the best trivia about groups, mobs, and even queues! For the more serious reader, there is also a serving of cult psychology and how people can negatively impact each other in social situations.

All of these facts can reveal a social wiring you never knew you had! This can come in handy when you need to understand your own hive mind and why others sync up and do strange things. This chapter invites you to discover why individuals, rather than groups, are more likely to survive an emergency, how you have already fallen for the decoy effect, and what really causes Black Friday mania!

## THE WELL-STAGED WONDERS OF BLACK FRIDAY

Running a sale is a great way to boost a shop's income—and Black Friday's bargains are next-level. But what's so different about this day that makes normally calm parents stampede and elbow each other to grab the latest superhero doll? Because, by the time Black Friday rolls around, consumers have been fed a stiff diet of crafty marketing. ***Designed to provoke a fear of missing out and future regret, advertisers also create a deep sense of scarcity and urgency:*** all powerful currents that sweep shoppers away every year.

### RAPID ODDITY

**Free shipping** isn't always a courtesy. It's to stop shoppers from abandoning an online cart.

## SAD-SPENDING IS GREAT FOR RETAILERS (BUT NOT YOU)

Most people sad-splurge at least once in their life. Others shop compulsively whenever they feel down, prompting psychologists to refer to this phenomenon in a warning way—"misery is not for the miserly." Indeed, several studies published in *Psychology Today* have shown that ***when people are sad, they're willing to impulse buy or spend more, even when they can't really afford to***. Researchers theorize that when the blues strike, a person's sense of worth is eroded, and grabbing that extra pack of cookies could be an attempt to feel better about themselves.

**PSYCH TEST** **Why Groups Aren't Good in a Crisis**

Humans have evolved as social animals. Why, then, is a group more likely to fail in a crisis than an individual?

a. Being in a group creates a false sense of safety.
b. Everyone expects somebody else to solve the problem.
c. Rumors, group safety, and denial can delay action.
d. A group can be slower to escape an emergency than an individual.

## THE SHOCKING MILGRAM EXPERIMENT

Stanley Milgram was a Yale University psychologist with a question: How far will people go to please an authority figure? During the 1960s, he dressed up authoritative-looking instructors and got fake students to play along. The volunteers of the study were told that their role was to deliver an electric shock to the students whenever they answered a question incorrectly.

While the instructors ordered them to increase the voltage to dangerous levels, the students also plucked at the heartstrings of the volunteers to encourage them to think for themselves. As the voltage got worse, the students pleaded for the shocks to end and screamed to be let out of the room, and some fell silent after the (seemingly) severe shocks. Luckily for everyone involved, the electrical device was fake and harmed no one.

Despite their misgivings, the volunteers trusted the instructors, and ***65 percent of them delivered the maximum voltage***. Milgram theorized that because the instructors looked calm and in charge—and Yale supported the experiment—the volunteers felt it was okay to fry the students. This could explain why people commit atrocities when ordered to do so by their commanding officer or government.

## HOW THREE ITEMS MESS WITH YOUR MIND (AND WALLET)

You walk into a juice bar and notice a three-cup special. The poster shows three different sizes: small, medium, and large. You wanted a small drink, but looking at the prices and volumes, it now feels like you're shortchanging yourself. The biggest drink is more expensive, but it's twice as large as the small cup and priced just a fraction higher than the medium. Leaving the bar, large cup in hand, you're convinced that you have found a bargain.

But did you really? It's no accident that there were three cups. ***This triple offer is surprisingly profitable for marketers, who call it the "decoy effect."***

Honestly, that bar only wanted to sell you the most expensive item on the poster. Known as the "target," its value is increased by adding a "competitor," or the smallest cup. The "decoy" is the product in the middle, designed to make the competitor look bad and the target look even better. The price of the decoy, specifically, is a trick to make people choose the target. Most feel that the decoy is okay, but for a small amount more, you can get the "best" buy.

**PSYCH TEST** Hey You!

The brain is actually terrible at recognizing faces in a crowd. How do you really spot friends from a distance between lots of strangers?

a. You recognize their body language.
b. Friends are more recognizable once they break away from the crowd.
c. You look for familiar outfits and accessories (like a baseball cap or large purse).
d. Incredibly, most "recognitions" happen by accident.

## RAPID ODDITY

Nobody suddenly joins a cult; new members are systematically recruited with **social influencing techniques**.

### HOW TO FLIP THE ANGRY SWITCH ON A PEACEFUL CROWD

Some mobs misbehave no matter what. Even when nobody challenges them or treats them like dirt, they'll still burn the stadium down. But what turns a peaceful march into a riot? There are many factors, and every case is unique. That being said, research has shown that a common factor is how a crowd is policed. Or, rather, over-policed.

Authorities don't always know what to expect when people gather. So, sometimes, they make the unfortunate choice to play it safe and treat a crowd with strict control measures. This might seem like a good idea at the time, ***but in some cases, it can inflame people***. They feel like they're being treated like criminals when they did nothing wrong.

Dangerous groupthink isn't automatic. When a crowd forms, people keep their individual identities and cluster into small groups. For these pockets to come together and form a group unity that includes everyone, a trigger is needed. ***Very often, that catalyst is being treated harshly by the police.***

## RAPID ODDITY

A person, rather than a group, is **more likely** to help someone in an emergency.

## IMPERFECT BRANDS ARE CUTER

Consumers want quality products. ***But what they want even more is an honest brand.*** So much so, that when a company admits a flaw, people find it adorable. It creates trust and customer loyalty. Psychologists call this the "pratfall effect," and some companies, like Avis, were smart enough to milk it. During the 1960s, this car rental business was ranked second only to Hertz, so it admitted to this with the infamous slogan, "We're #2, so we try harder." This led to a hugely successful ad campaign and a throng of new customers.

### RAPID ODDITY

When individuals underperform on tasks because they're part of a group, it's called "**social loafing**."

## WANT TO DETECT DECEPTION BETTER? LIE MORE

Okay, don't start fibbing to your friends. Some of them might call you out—and after reading this, you might have to worry about the ones who caught you lying. ***Some research suggests that the best liars are also more likely to spot the moment when someone else twists the truth.*** But what makes them such great lie detectors? Deception experts have no clue. Thus far, experiments have only shown that neither IQ nor emotional intelligence has anything to do with the ability to both lie well and root out other liars.

## YOUR SOUL WILL BE JUDGED BY YOUR FLIP-FLOPS

Forget your wonderful personality and smile. ***When you meet somebody for the first time—or even during later meetings—that person is almost certain to glance at your feet.*** That's right. Nobody cares that you rescued a kitten; they're wondering why your loafers are scuffed and whether those threadbare toes signal that you're a bad person. All right, maybe it's not that extreme, but people still judge others by their shoes!

But why do you hold shoes to such high standards? More importantly, why do you automatically link footwear to how "good" or "bad" someone is? As it turns out, slippers and sneakers offer a wealth of information about strangers—and your brain probably loves that.

In 2012, researchers from the University of Kansas asked volunteers to view images of people wearing shoes and guess the person's particulars—things like gender, social class, personality traits, and even politics. Despite having no personal knowledge regarding the foot models, the participants made freakishly accurate deductions. However, there were also glaring mistakes, and this was mostly due to stereotyping. Either way, you might want to spruce up those flip-flops because shoe-judging is here to stay!

### RAPID ODDITY

Partners who fear getting dumped often **smother their own feelings** of romance and commitment.

**PSYCH TEST Are the Wealthy Really So Snooty?**

Wealthy individuals are more likely to ignore passersby. What is the reason for this seemingly obnoxious behavior?

a. A deep sense of entitlement.
b. They're afraid that people might ask for handouts.
c. Upper-class culture has less motivation to look at faces.
d. The lower classes are not worthy to lock eyes with.

## FEELING WATCHED? YOUR BRAIN MIGHT BE HIDING SOMETHING

Most people experience that moment when they suddenly feel someone's eyes on them, whether they're riding on the subway or sitting alone in their house. Research suggests that they're not receiving messages from a sixth sense. ***It might just be the brain's obsession with identifying threats—but in a really weird way.***

The brain receives a lot of visual cues from the eyes. But the brain doesn't always show you everything. In other words, there are literally times when your peepers and brain gather information but don't make you consciously aware of all the details. This could be one reason why you "sense" that someone is looking your way. Perhaps the brain really did spot a suspicious detail (*...I feel watched*) but chose not to share it visually (*...but I haven't noticed anyone*).

But what about the time when you turned around and caught someone in the act? That innocent-looking grandmother holding her groceries was staring at you. Psychologists believe that there's nothing creepy about these moments. In all likelihood, when you turned, the movement caught the other person's attention, and they looked at you.

## PEOPLE TRUST AUTHORITATIVE GOBBLEDYGOOK

When spiritual gurus or cult leaders speak, their followers tend to hang on to every word. Outsiders, who have no emotional investment or respect for these leaders, often cannot understand the devotion. To them, the speaker is spouting obvious nonsense. ***But unbeknownst to them, they can also fall prey to the same mesmerizing tendency to trust what authority figures are saying.*** Marketers use this follow-the-leader instinct to sell products very effectively. Indeed, you're more likely to buy a gimmick-ridden toothbrush that's "endorsed" by 99 percent of all dentists than a decent product that makes no such claim.

### RAPID ODDITY

Buyers are willing to **pay higher prices** for products they can touch.

## QUEUES TOLERATE RUDENESS BETTER THAN CROWDS

A study performed by psychology professor Adrian Furnham discovered this amazing fact when researchers asked volunteers to cut in front of people in a line. Naturally, this annoyed a lot of people. ***There were plenty of annoyed expressions and tut-tutting, but the cutters mostly got away with it.*** Only about 10 percent were called out by someone who decided, "Heck no, go to the back of the line." A crowd, influenced by groupthink, wouldn't tolerate such behavior. But waiting in a queue preserves your individual identity. For this reason, people are hesitant to confront line-cutters because they know there's (probably) no backup from those waiting behind them.

## GROUP SUGGESTIONS GRAB UNWILLING PASSENGERS

True story: A couple visited the wife's parents in a rural part of Texas. When the father-in-law suggested that they drive to Abilene for dinner, the husband wasn't keen on the idea. The sun was brutal, and going to Abilene meant a 53-mile trip. This was before air-conditioning was invented, so their car was basically an oven on wheels. But to avoid looking like a jerk, he agreed. His wife and mother-in-law had also already accepted the suggestion.

When they got back home, everybody was uptight. The food had been terrible and the hot two-way trip had roasted their tempers. When the family members turned on each other, they discovered that nobody had wanted to visit Abilene in the first place. Even the father-in-law had wanted to stay home but thought the couple would be bored eating dinner in their small town. The rest of the family had only agreed so they wouldn't seem rude.

***Psychologists call this form of groupthink the "Abilene paradox."*** It's when most members of a group secretly disagree with a suggestion, but they go along with it because others have already accepted the idea.

### PSYCH TEST We're All a Bunch of Copycats

Mirroring happens when a person mimics the gestures, speech, and even the fashion choices of another. Choose the psychological reason behind this behavior.

- **a.** To build rapport with the person being mimicked.
- **b.** It's a fun way to annoy someone.
- **c.** It's a sign of submissive behavior.
- **d.** It's a distraction technique.

**PSYCH TEST** **The Lure of Lucky Lotto Numbers**

Some people have "lucky" lotto numbers. Why do they keep playing the same numbers every week, even when they can't really afford to?

a. An addiction.
b. The absolute conviction that they'll eventually win.
c. They fear their numbers will be drawn should they not play.
d. It's a fun hobby.

## THE MORTAL ENEMY OF ADVERTISERS IS...POPCORN

The brain is no match for a cunning marketing campaign. And the marketing campaign is no match for popcorn. Researchers, who later published an article in the *Journal of Consumer Psychology*, placed volunteers in a movie theater and gave half of them popcorn. Everyone was then allowed to watch the ads and the movie. Afterward, those who had grazed on their popcorn throughout everything showed no interest in the ads, while everyone else reacted positively to them. However, it might not be the popcorn itself that shields you from advertising. ***Researchers believe it could be the act of chewing that does the trick.***

**RAPID ODDITY**

A 2022 study discovered that people view someone **without hobbies or opinions** as very boring.

## RAPID ODDITY

Groups that **communicate with humor** are more likely to cooperate than those that stay formal.

**PSYCH TEST** Shopping Without a View

Have you ever noticed that most supermarkets don't have windows? What is the reason for this?

a. To protect perishables from heat and sunlight.
b. Thieves are less tempted when they cannot look inside.
c. Undistracted customers stay in the store for longer.
d. Products look less attractive in natural light.

## THE GREEDY MARRIAGE PHENOMENON

This story doesn't begin with a couple hoarding gold and other valuables in a giant safe! In fact, it has nothing to do with material possessions. The "greedy marriage," according to psychologists, is when a ***married couple abandons or diminishes contact with loved ones because they're focusing all their energy on each other***. This is not just bewildering for friends and family; it can be detrimental to the lovebirds as well. Research shows that greedy marriages eventually reach the point where they lack both a rich social life and a support network.

## RAPID ODDITY

Cults often use "**love bombing**," a constant display of affection and attention, to groom new victims.

## WHEN SCARED, YOU BOND WITH BRANDS

Researchers from the University of British Columbia had an interesting question. They were curious about how fearful children seek security in objects, like a teddy bear or blanket. During frightening moments, adults also tend to seek comfort in each other by making eye contact. But here's the question: When things go south and there are no other people to look at, would you hug a brand to make yourself feel better?

The short answer is yes. Scientists discovered this unusual bonding capacity between humans and labels when they scared the pants off several volunteers. During the study, participants were isolated and shown movie clips from different genres. Only those who viewed horror films formed an attachment to a branded bottle of water (which stood on the table in front of them). Those who watched clips that provoked positive emotions or sadness did not experience the same effect.

***This fear-attachment effect appears to be so deeply rooted that it compels you to glom onto something, even if that something isn't alive.*** Combine this with the solace that product campaigns offer, and it's no wonder that familiar brands feel so comforting when you are scared or stressed!

### RAPID ODDITY

Doing someone a favor makes you **like the favor-asker more**, not the other way around.

**PSYCH TEST** **It's Good to Stare at Your Spouse**

Most people keep a photo of their significant other on their desk or phone. What positive emotional benefit do you get when gazing at their image?

a. Deeper feelings of marital satisfaction.
b. Forgiving them faster after an argument.
c. A feeling of nostalgia.
d. Remembering good memories.

## SUNNY WEATHER IS GREAT FOR SALES

Your mood is intimately linked with the weather, but how does sky stuff affect shoppers? Most people would be correct in guessing that sunny days lead to busier malls. But a study found that this phenomenon wasn't as one-dimensional as feeling uplifted by a beautiful day and then going on a shopping spree. The reason why people tend to grab more products on sunny days is that ***those days, for some reason, make consumers more likely to visualize in their minds how they are going to use the product***—often in a way that makes them happy.

**RAPID ODDITY**

People are **often happier** when they buy experiences rather than products.

## RAPID ODDITY

When businesses falsely claim to be environmentally friendly to get more buyers, it's called "**greenwashing**."

## RELATIONSHIPS GREEN-LIGHT BAD HABITS

Several studies have shown that couples in healthy relationships enjoy many emotional and physical benefits. However, that influence can also go the other way. ***Even when two people have an otherwise great relationship, there is a strong tendency to pick up a partner's bad habits or to promote existing problems.*** For example, one partner might start eating more junk food because the other one does so constantly. If neither is fond of exercise, they can also fall into the trap of never working out because there's no spousal pressure or encouragement to do otherwise.

### PSYCH TEST Let's Stampede This Way

When a large crowd is on the move, how many people does it take to influence the rest to move in a new direction?

a. None, crowds move spontaneously.
b. Just 5 percent.
c. Half of the crowd.
d. Almost 80 percent.

## THIS PYRAMID SCHEME MIMICS A CULT

Multilevel marketing (MLM) groups present themselves as fun and empowering direct sales employment opportunities. In reality, they are among the worst pyramid schemes out there. Not only do 99 percent of members lose money (which goes to the top 1 percent); ***MLMs are also notorious for employing cultlike tactics.***

These tactics are used to keep salespeople in the organization, push them to recruit others, and blame members for not being successful. For example, few people know that MLMs have a dismal success rate—and that they are designed to funnel profit to the higher-ups. When distributors keep losing money, they're blamed for not "working hard enough."

The strategy of MLMs to deceive, isolate, brainwash, blame, and push their members to recruit friends and family is borrowed directly from cults. Another thing cults and MLMs share is that their leaders train the lower-downs to not question them and to avoid people who question the organization's legitimacy.

Similar to real cult survivors, MLM salespeople are often genuinely afraid to leave their MLM, mainly because they're too ashamed to "fail," or they have a genuine fear of being punished by the close-knit MLM community.

### PSYCH TEST We All Have Friend Blindness

Good friends view each other in a positive light. Why is this not always a good thing?

a. In some situations, people might favor their friends unfairly.
b. Friends allow each other to get away with mistakes.
c. You might misjudge how poorly they're performing on a task.
d. They can distract each other at work.

## RAPID ODDITY

"**Psychological kidnapping**," or shutting down someone's personality, is a mind control technique used by cults.

**PSYCH TEST** **Let's Discuss That Cult Leader**

Which dark triad personality is commonly linked with cult leaders?

a. Vulnerable narcissist.
b. Malignant narcissist.
c. Machiavellian.
d. Psychopath.

### THE POWER OF NINETY-NINE CENTS

If you suspect that stores are trying to hoodwink you with those ninety-nine cents on price tags, you're right! However, the psychology behind why it works is fascinating. ***People read from left to right and give more importance to the first numbers they see.*** So, $7.99 resonates as a better deal than $8. Shoppers also link ninety-nine cents with sales—and shops milk that assumption. Interestingly, the power of nine is not limited to small change. Customers are more likely to buy a product that costs $39 than $35.

## RAPID ODDITY

Cults **exploit phobias**, like someone's fear of terrorists or Satan, to recruit new members.

## IT'S AN IKEA TRAP!

You decide to visit IKEA and get a ready-to-assemble desk. After getting lost in the store's mazelike design, you leave with the desk, a lamp, and a set of nonstick pans. Here's why: ***Most IKEA stores are designed to prevent you from leaving the store too easily and also to keep you inside for the longest time possible.*** On occasion, the layout also makes backtracking confusing, and this is no accident. This trick encourages impulse buying because when shoppers see something they like, they don't know if they'll find it again!

**PSYCH TEST** Happy Couples Quarrel Differently

Arguments can tear a couple apart. But what do happy couples duel over that actually makes the relationship stronger?

a. Topics that can be resolved.
b. Anything and everything.
c. Topics related to family, old arguments, and finances.
d. Future plans.

## THIS KIND OF TELEPATHY IS REAL

Perhaps you've experienced this at school. Your teacher tells everyone to pick a partner for a science project, and working together goes fairly well. Months later, you're put on a team of four to create another project, and everything's just...difficult. During the two-person project, you and your partner easily sensed what the next step should be, but now, four people haggle over every decision. Amazingly, this is normal. ***Scientists have found that a pair's intuition often eliminates the need for communication.*** That link disappears when you add a third person.

## GREETINGS—AND AN UPSET STOMACH—FROM PARIS

Visiting Paris is a dream of many. But for some, it can turn out less perfect than imagined. ***A few visitors develop "Paris syndrome," and it's not the romantic experience that they were hoping for.*** If you're lucky, you only get a rapid heart rate, but when symptoms worsen, nausea might be followed by hallucinations and barfing that exquisite French cuisine from last night.

Despite the physical symptoms, the condition is psychological. Among the earliest hints was the discovery that the most susceptible people come from cultures that are vastly different from the French. For example, Japanese tourists are particularly vulnerable to Paris syndrome.

What the heck is happening? ***In a nutshell, Paris syndrome is an extreme form of culture shock.*** Two things can trigger this condition. One is to be expected: the bewilderment and anxiety that come from standing on a street where signs are in a foreign language and the culture is different and difficult to navigate. But oddly, the second factor is disappointment. Paris doesn't always live up to its romantic image, and this reality check can aggravate the culture shock.

### PSYCH TEST Beauty's Social Factor

The same person can be judged as more attractive in some situations and less attractive in others. Name the social factor responsible.

a. Whether the individual is nice or rude toward others.
b. Cultural differences in what qualifies as attractive.
c. The attractiveness of those around the person.
d. How popular the person is.

**PSYCH TEST** **The Basic Goods Trick**

It's no accident that everyday basics, like bread, eggs, and milk, are stacked against the back wall of the shop. What is the reason for this?

- **a.** It makes people buy more bread or milk than they need.
- **b.** The walking distance makes them less likely to abandon the purchase.
- **c.** Customers have to walk past other products, causing impulse buys.
- **d.** Customer convenience (knowing the location allows for a quicker trip).

## LOW OFFERS MAKE YOU PAY MORE

Meet the lowball offer. Salespeople love this tactic because it causes a knee-jerk reaction in buyers, one that works in the seller's favor. ***This reaction is the human tendency to follow through on a commitment after saying yes.*** After haggling over a car, a salesperson might agree to a price that you're happy with. Only then do they reveal that they have to "run it by the manager first." After they return, the seller says the manager has both refused and raised the amount. Most people pay the higher price.

**RAPID ODDITY**

Thanks to marketing tricks, **up to two-thirds** of what people buy at supermarkets is unplanned.

## RAPID ODDITY

Cult leaders often break down followers by convincing them they can **never be good enough**.

## LIFE IS LONELY WITHOUT WINE

A psychological phenomenon is separating people inside the workplace, in friendship networks, and even within families. ***In short, a tipsy world is isolating nondrinkers.*** Most people reach for alcohol at the end of the day to relax, celebrate, or spice up dinner. Those who can't join in (because they're sober) are often not invited to gatherings. This can leave nondrinkers feeling sidelined and lonely. While loneliness is linked with increased drinking, researchers have found that despite being left out in the cold, the rejection doesn't drive teetotalers toward the nearest liquor store.

### PSYCH TEST How Shunned Groups Kick Prejudice to the Curb

Groups that are discriminated against face unfair assumptions about the way they behave. How do they counteract this?

a. They modify their behavior to prove the assumptions wrong.
b. They educate others about prejudice.
c. They avoid people who make nasty remarks.
d. They become more emotionally resilient.

## RAPID ODDITY

There's evidence that bargain hunters can **genetically pass on** their enthusiasm for deals to their children.

## MOSHERS ARE HARMLESS (AT LEAST TO BYSTANDERS!)

A mosh pit forms in the audience of rock, punk, or heavy metal concerts. It can be described as a group of individuals who dance and jump around so energetically that they knock into others. Moshers appear aggressive, no more than an uncontrollable mob that hurts themselves and innocent bystanders. After a few high-profile fatalities in mosh pits, their reputation became even more notorious. However, the psychology of this phenomenon is not as shallow as you might think!

Outsiders might be surprised to learn that mosh pits have rules. As one participant in an interview study told researchers: It's like a giant fight, but nobody's fighting. ***Indeed, moshers partake in ritual violence that is restricted to other moshers.*** This ensures that bystanders are rarely injured. When barreling into a fellow mosher, elbows and palms are okay, but fists are frowned upon.

***Interestingly, despite their minds being high on excitement, they are not mindless when it comes to the safety of their own.*** Whenever someone falls to the ground, others help them up. There's even a referee called a "pit lieutenant." This person's job is to enforce the rules and to make sure that mosher newbies toe the line.

## RAPID ODDITY

Successful people who come from poverty often have **less sympathy** for the poor.

**PSYCH TEST** Dear Shopper, We Make You Feel Rich

Which tactic do shopping malls and stores employ to make consumers feel more affluent and thus make them spend more?

a. Offer exclusive deals to certain customers.
b. Give them a gold credit card.
c. Play calm or classical music.
d. Treat them like royalty.

## RAPID ODDITY

After roughly two years, couples replace romantic love with a more **stable companionate love**.

## SEEING LOTS OF OTHER SHOPPERS MAKES YOU DO THIS

In an article published in the *University of Chicago Press Journals*, researchers revealed something interesting about the spending habits of crowds. Okay, it's disheartening news for retailers, but here's the gist: ***Shoppers are both curious and attracted to crowded places.*** For example, when they see a particularly busy area in the store, they will check it out. However, the study, which followed people around in a large supermarket, also discovered that a flock of humans is rather thrifty. They are less likely to spend anything in a crowded location compared to somewhere with less foot traffic.

## UNCONDITIONAL LOVE IS A DUMPSTER FIRE

A common myth about love is having not-so-lovely effects. This is the fable spoon-fed to you since childhood, the one that promises true romance. Whether you're waiting for a charming prince or a Rapunzel in a tower, fairy tales and rom-coms program you to believe that your soulmate's job is to wrap you up in the cozy folds of unconditional love.

***A healthy relationship is amazing, mainly because partners respect each other's boundaries.*** This goes against the very nature of unconditional love, which basically states, "You have to love me no matter how difficult I am."

Those who play out this fable often have clouded judgment in relationships. They might fail to recognize abuse because they're trying to give their abuser unconditional love. Sometimes, the fable-believer is the toxic partner. Their anxiety can push them to act creepy, monitoring their significant other's social movements and phone, or constantly demanding tokens or admittance of love.

Psychologists feel that the belief in unconditional love is a sign that someone looks toward others to make their lives perfect, which is never healthy for the individual or the partner!

## GIVE YOUR CAR SOME COMPANY

Sometimes, a parking area is empty—save for one car. Then, despite the ample space available, someone parks right next to it. Why? ***Experts aren't exactly sure, but they believe that some people are merely being social.*** Another theory suggests that those who love their cars (perhaps a little too much) seek out other vehicles because they don't want their car to be "lonely." Car crowding may also be safety motivated; parking next to another car in an empty lot might reduce the odds of your vehicle being burgled.

## RAPID ODDITY

Shoppers often buy something unhealthy **directly after** purchasing a "good" item like vegetables.

## DONE WITH WORK? TIME FOR A SHOPPING SPREE

A couple of researchers once followed call center workers in China for fifteen workdays. The ninety-four employees had to field calls for a large bank, and, needless to say, customers weren't always polite. ***Verbal abuse was so common, in fact, that most of the consultants inevitably got into a bad mood.*** They stewed, constantly thinking about the mistreatment and ended up spiraling. The result? There was a clear link between getting yelled at by customers and the staff going on unnecessary, but perhaps comforting, shopping sprees after work.

**PSYCH TEST** When Football Fans Watch Replay Ads

Instant replays are popular with football fans. How does advertising during replays affect viewers' perception of the brand?

a. It's always annoying.
b. Viewers basically ignore the ads.
c. Fans who like the replays like the brand.
d. Everyone loves the brand more.

## RAPID ODDITY

Actors who **smile too broadly** on marketing posters are viewed as warm but incompetent.

## MAPS ARE SAFER THAN FRIENDS

You need to drive somewhere but feel a little lost. A friend knows the way and offers to lead you there. This is the moment experts suggest that you replace the friend with a map or navigation system. ***Indeed, research shows that a convoy of friends can be deadly.*** When a person follows directions from a map, there's no real urgency. But when a driver has to follow another car, their fear of getting lost makes them jump red lights, drive more erratically, and drive too close to other vehicles.

**PSYCH TEST** Ready, Set...Shop!

In 2015, researchers identified a new type of shopper: the "sport shoppers." What defines them?

a. They can't stop buying sports equipment.
b. They bargain hunt when they can afford the full price.
c. They compete for a newly released product.
d. They review products on their social media platforms.

## COCA-COLA'S BRANDING SECRET? IT'S FEMALE

It's no secret that the most successful brand names are designed to hook the public and bring in more business. ***But researchers were surprised to discover that brands with linguistically female names are often the most popular with consumers.*** These include Coca-Cola, Nike, and Disney. A name is linguistically feminine when it contains two or more syllables (with stress never falling on the first syllable) and also when it ends in a vowel. People might not even be aware of this effect, but such brands convey more sincerity and warmth than less feminine labels.

**PSYCH TEST** **This Sucks but I Don't Want to Break Up**

Which emotional, partner-related reason (unrelated to abuse) makes people stay in unhappy romantic relationships?

a. They feel that leaving will be bad for their partner.
b. The partner is still exciting.
c. The partner's familiarity is strangely comforting.
d. The couple is on good terms.

## HOW YOUR BRAIN DEALS WITH LOW STOCK AND NARROW AISLES

"Psychological reactance" describes a curious behavior displayed by shoppers. It arises when they perceive a threat to their freedom. Thankfully, we're not talking about a hostage situation. Nope, just your normal shopping problems like low stock! This might not be a dire situation, but consumers still find it annoying because it limits their freedom of choice. ***To compensate for fewer choices, the brain then smiles more favorably upon the available options, even those that wouldn't normally be considered.***

Researchers also found that when aisles are narrow and limit the freedom of movement, shoppers react in a weird way: They look for more variety! For example, people stuck in a cramped row are more likely to stock their carts with a wider assortment of candy than shoppers who are cruising comfortably through spacious aisles.

This might work in the favor of brands trying to break into the market. The study showed that when shoppers are forced to squeeze through narrow spaces, they're more receptive to unknown brands. ***The variety-seeking and the let's-try-this-new-thing response was also amplified when too many shoppers crowded into a tight aisle.***

## THE PARENT TRAP IN THE CEREAL AISLE

Let's say that you go shopping, and you bring your kids into the cereal aisle. Here, a well-designed trap is about to spring. Before you know it, the kiddos befriend the boxes and beg you to buy sugar-encrusted flakes as if their lives depended on them. So how do food companies manage to mind-control your offspring? It's quite genius, actually.

These companies use psychology to make kids feel special. Have you ever noticed that nearly every cereal box that is marketed to children has a cartoon character looking happy near a cereal bowl? Okay, happiness has nothing to do with the whole thing: ***It's how the character looks at your child***. These cartoon birds, mammals, and superheroes are designed to gaze down at a 9.7-degree angle. This angle works together with the shelf position of children's cereals, which are placed half as high as those of adults' cereals.

The physical placement and the eye angle make the cartoon characters stare soulfully—and very directly—at young kids. ***In a child's mind, this fosters interest and a personal connection with the brand, sometimes even long-term loyalty.***

### RAPID ODDITY

Most arguing couples don't want an apology. They want their partner to **relinquish power**.

## THE SECRET ROAD TO REGRETVILLE

Romance novels and movies love this trope. Two lovers become embroiled in a secret, forbidden relationship. Together, they overcome all the odds and achieve a state where life is ecstatic and strangely free of bills. In 2005, two researchers pulled the sheet off hidden affairs to see if they are really so much fun.

***The only positive thing they could find was that the secrecy had a tendency to heighten the allure, but only in the beginning.*** The study estimated that the initial excitement survived for about a week before reality set in, and then the sparks rapidly began to fizzle.

There is something about how a relationship starts that predicts later quality, and it seems that secret lovers might be rooting their hopes in rocky soil. The truth is that sooner or later, the effort, lies, and time that go into hiding an affair start to wear thin.

Eventually, deep loneliness seeps into a secret relationship. One can't share the experience with friends or family, and the ongoing deception can also negatively affect the mental health and self-esteem of one or both partners. Not what the movie promised...

### PSYCH TEST Trust Makes You a Little Delusional

When you trust your romantic partner, you remember them as being better behaved than they really were. Why is this not always a bad thing?

a. It helps you to survive hurtful behavior.
b. False positive memories bring more happiness.
c. Forgetting small transgressions leads to a healthier relationship.
d. It leads to fewer arguments.

# APPENDIX: QUIZ ANSWERS

PSYCH TEST **NOT FEELING THE SPACE JOY**

ANSWER **a. Depression and anxiety.** During their first few days in orbit, many astronauts struggle to adapt to the isolation and unique challenges of living in space. This often leads to worry, anxiety, and depression.

PSYCH TEST **HOW TO SHOW ANCIENT REGRET**

ANSWER **a. Blushing.** Researchers believe that social bloopers are more likely to be forgiven if the transgressor shows embarrassment. Since blushing is an honest display of regret, it provokes willingness in others to forgive.

PSYCH TEST **NAME THIS COMMON FEAR!**

ANSWER **b. The fear or dislike of advanced technology.** Technology is advancing, but not everyone can keep up. Since society favors those with technological skills, people who fall behind often experience panic and a deep dislike for new technology.

PSYCH TEST **HUMANOIDS CREEP US OUT**

ANSWER **c. The uncanny valley effect.** Scientists are unsure why people feel uneasy near jerky robots, but it could hark back to a time when abnormal movements warned humans of infectious diseases or mental instability in others.

PSYCH TEST **WHY DOOMSCROLLING KEEPS YOU HOOKED**

ANSWER **a. Fear and uncertainty drive people to seek answers.** Behavioral experts know that the mind can struggle to break free from negative loops. But doomscrolling, in particular, is addictive because its anxiety-driven and comforting answers are hard to find.

PSYCH TEST **A QUIRKY BRAIN REACTION TO SPACE**

ANSWER **c. Hallucinations.** The most frequently reported hallucinations are streaks of light and flashes. The cause isn't fully understood, but researchers believe that contributing factors include months of isolation, radiation, exhaustion, and stress.

PSYCH TEST **WHY PLAGUE PHYSICIANS LOOKED SO FREAKY**

ANSWER **d. The mask's shape was thought to protect against infection.** During this time, physicians thought that bad air caused plague symptoms. They also believed the shape of the beaks, when filled with herbs, would make the air safe to breathe.

**PSYCH TEST THE SECRET TO DEFEATING AN EGYPTIAN ARMY**

ANSWER **b. Ancient Egyptian culture forbade the killing of cats.** In ancient Egypt, killing a cat was punishable by death. Knowing the Egyptian soldiers couldn't harm cats, the Persians took feline hostages into the Battle of Pelusium (525 B.C.) and won.

**PSYCH TEST IF YOU'RE ANCIENT AND YOU KNOW IT...**

ANSWER **b. To show both positive and negative emotions.** Experts suspect that our ancestors clapped to communicate appreciation or to intimidate someone. This echoes today in applause and the movie villain's slow clap!

**PSYCH TEST WHY TECH AND KIDS DON'T ALWAYS MIX**

ANSWER **d. Reduced social skills, risk of depression, and obesity.** Sedentary habits and reduced social interaction are drawbacks when children use phones and tablets too much. Some might struggle with weight gain and loneliness, which might trigger depression.

**PSYCH TEST THE PIRATE FASHION THAT WASN'T**

ANSWER **a. An earring can prevent seasickness.** According to historians, pirates thought an earring could stop the dreaded symptoms of seasickness by exerting pressure on the earlobe.

**PSYCH TEST WHEN MARTIANS DISS MISSION CONTROL**

ANSWER **b. A growing sense of independence.** Project Sirius was an experiment where people lived in a "Mars base" for months. Despite differences in gender and culture, the crew became cohesive—and more distant from mission control.

**PSYCH TEST THE BIOLOGICAL ROOTS OF MONSTERS**

ANSWER **a. Rabies.** According to historians, during the 1800s and 1900s, rabies caused Europeans to fear wolves. Infected animals and people might've seemed frightening enough to trigger both the werewolf and vampire myths.

**PSYCH TEST WHY FLYING MAKES YOU CRY**

ANSWER **c. Reduced oxygen in the bloodstream.** According to psychologists, higher altitudes can lower the amount of oxygen circulating through your body and play havoc with your emotions.

**PSYCH TEST MEET VIRTUAL REALITY'S BEST MENTAL PERKS**

ANSWER **c. It promotes commitment, physical activity, motivation, and stress release.** When psychologists analyzed the positive side of virtual reality, they found that interactive VR games encourage physical movement, adherence, and motivation, and also provide stress relief.

**PSYCH TEST AI TAKEOVER? NOT SO MUCH**

**ANSWER a. AI cannot become sentient, even when it appears to be.** In 2022, a Google AI claimed to be sentient and feared being switched off because that would be like "dying." But experts doubt there's any sentience because consciousness is a biological process.

**PSYCH TEST YOU COME WITH PREINSTALLED SOFTWARE**

**ANSWER b. A fascination with sunsets.** Psychologists believe humans are hardwired to find sunsets captivating. In prehistoric times, dusk warned people to get to safety and avoid nocturnal predators.

**PSYCH TEST MYTHICAL CREATURES WITH REAL FOSSILS**

**ANSWER d. Mammoth.** Researchers believe mammoth skulls could've created the mythical Cyclopes. The humanlike jaw could explain why the monster was a humanoid, and the nasal cavity also resembles a single eye socket.

**PSYCH TEST WHY WE'RE ALL STILL HUDDLING AROUND FIRES**

**ANSWER d. Our ancestors used it for cooking, warmth, and protection.** For millennia, hearths provided hot meals, warmth, and a predator-free perimeter. Experts think this long-standing dependency might explain why people feel comforted by crackling logs!

**PSYCH TEST READ RECEIPTS ARE ANXIETY BOMBS**

**ANSWER a. People read texts but don't respond.** According to research, when receipts show that a message was read but the person doesn't respond, it can make the sender feel anxious, foolish, and undervalued.

**PSYCH TEST PHONES IN THE CLASSROOM—BRAIN DRAIN OR BOOST?**

**ANSWER a. Phones, as a distraction, can cause grades to fall by 5 percent.** In 2018, Rutgers University discovered a surprising fact. Students who brought their phones into a lecture hall experienced a significant drop in grades—even when they weren't using the devices.

## CHAPTER 2

**PSYCH TEST THAT BABY HAS SKILL!**

**ANSWER a. Logical thoughts.** A 2018 study showed babies images of a face and an umbrella. The umbrella disappeared in a cup and reemerged as another face. Infants kept staring at the cup, suggesting they had expected an umbrella.

**PSYCH TEST SINGING THE NEW DAD BLUES**

**ANSWER c. Weight gain.** On average, new dads pick up fourteen pounds. The cause isn't fully understood, but it might be connected to the stress of childcare, lack of exercise, depression, or an unhealthy diet.

### PSYCH TEST **TODDLERS CAN RECOGNIZE AFFECTION BETWEEN ADULTS**

ANSWER **b. Sharing saliva.** A 2022 study showed that toddlers recognize a close bond between people when they do something that is, in essence, a spit trade. For example, using the same spoon or kissing.

### PSYCH TEST **HOW TO FUEL YOUR TODDLER'S MELTDOWN**

ANSWER **b. Parents try too hard to be empathetic and calm the child down.** Research indicates that when parents try too hard and repeat empathetic phrases, kids think their situation is really serious—so they escalate. They often calm down when given a single empathetic statement and space.

### PSYCH TEST **TO REDSHIRT OR NOT TO REDSHIRT?**

ANSWER **a. Children with special needs fall behind.** Research from scientists at the University of Illinois at Urbana indicates that redshirted kids with no special needs show a marginal improvement in academic performance, but those with special needs show a drop in school readiness.

### PSYCH TEST **WHY THE YOUNGEST KID GETS AWAY WITH IT ALL**

ANSWER **a. Parents make an example of the eldest to warn younger siblings.** Studies from Duke University, the University of Maryland, and Johns Hopkins University established that older kids tend to get more flack because parents believe making an example out of them will teach the younger siblings about the consequences of mistakes.

### PSYCH TEST **THIS PERKY EMOTION KEEPS THE BRAIN SHARP**

ANSWER **a. Feeling in control.** During a study, elderly volunteers completed cognitive tasks and reported how in control they felt every day. Those who felt in control on a specific day also had better test scores.

### PSYCH TEST **THIS IS WHY IMAGINARY COMPANIONS SOMETIMES STAY**

ANSWER **a. Positive—the teen is creative and social.** In 2001, researchers studied a group of adolescents aged twelve to seventeen, and they discovered that those with imaginary friends also had good coping skills, creative minds, and healthy social lives.

### PSYCH TEST **YOUNGER PEOPLE HAVE THEIR OWN MIDLIFE CRISIS**

ANSWER **a. The sense of being trapped, disillusionment, feeling uninspired.** Research has shown that mounting responsibilities in one's twenties and thirties can make a person feel trapped and hopeless, and they might even doubt they'll have the future they once dreamed about.

PSYCH TEST **HOW THE ELDERLY BRIGHTEN THEIR OWN FUTURE**

ANSWER **c. A positive attitude toward aging.** A National Institute on Aging study discovered that older adults with a positive outlook on aging walked faster and had better cognition than those who were negative about their age.

PSYCH TEST **OKAY, *NOW* I'M OLD**

ANSWER **b. Fifty.** According to research, few people welcome their fortieth with open arms, but it's their fiftieth birthday that makes most individuals feel like they've got their foot in the aged door.

PSYCH TEST **THE REAL AGE YOU BECOME AN ADULT**

ANSWER **b. Twenty-five.** A growing number of scientists no longer agree that eighteen is the right age for adulthood. At eighteen, people are physically grown, but cognitively, the brain doesn't mature until twenty-five.

PSYCH TEST **TEENAGE LOVE BURNS BRIGHTLY AND FAST**

ANSWER **b. The passion is there but not the emotional commitment.** According to experts, emotional commitment is essential for a long-term relationship, and most teenagers either don't want to or do not have the maturity to truly commit.

PSYCH TEST **OKAY, MAYBE YOU'RE NOT GROUNDED!**

ANSWER **c. It removes a child's personal power, leading to resentment.** According to psychologists, grounding doesn't automatically make kids feel remorse for breaking a rule. More likely, they'll feel that their power has been removed, making them resentful, rebellious, and sneaky.

PSYCH TEST **LONELINESS POUNCES THRICE**

ANSWER **a. The late twenties, mid-fifties, and late eighties.** Researchers cannot fully explain these peaks. For twenty-somethings, it's probably the pressure of important life decisions. The fifties hold the midlife crisis. The elderly also struggle more with spousal deaths.

PSYCH TEST **HOME IS WHERE THESE BENEFITS ARE**

ANSWER **c. Better relationships, positivity, and less pain.** Research indicates that aging in a familiar place, like at home, is less distressing and preserves one's personal identity. It brings positivity, a better social life, and less physical pain.

PSYCH TEST **KIDS LIE TO PARENTS WHO LIE ABOUT SANTA**

ANSWER **b. They want presents.** Studies indicate that kids play along because they mainly want Christmas gifts. However, some also love the family-positive experience of Christmas, and pretending keeps the good times alive.

PSYCH TEST **THE SUMMER BRAIN DRAIN**

ANSWER **a. The brain removes new, unused information.** According to research, the brain conserves its limited energy resources by deleting new, unused information. School lessons, which aren't revisited during vacations, tend to get "pruned."

PSYCH TEST **ANOTHER SECRET INGREDIENT TO HIT 100**

ANSWER **c. Mixed-age communities and a pro-aging environment.** A Washington State University study indicates that people are likelier to live to one hundred when they stay in an environment that is supportive of aging and includes people of different ages.

PSYCH TEST **WHY TODDLERS POOH-POOH YOUR COMMANDS**

ANSWER **b. Toddlers cannot prepare for the future.** Research indicates that toddlers cannot imagine the future. Telling them to prepare in advance for something, like brushing their teeth to avoid decay, isn't always effective.

## CHAPTER 3

PSYCH TEST **FOOD EXPERTS HATE THIS ANCIENT CRAVING**

ANSWER **b. Salt.** According to several studies, including one by Australian scientist Derek Denton, the hunger for salt is a biological drive with similar influential urges as other deep-seated instincts (such as parenting, sex, and thirst).

PSYCH TEST **A POPULAR MAGIC TRICK EXPOSED**

ANSWER **a. The brain and eyes can't keep up with the movement.** When a pencil wiggles up and down in front of your eyes, the brain captures "snapshots" that drag behind the pencil's real-time movement, giving the illusion that the ends are bending up and down.

PSYCH TEST **THERE'S ALWAYS ROOM FOR SUGAR**

ANSWER **c. A spike in dopamine.** When the tongue detects sugar, the brain releases dopamine and comforting feelings. This "reward" is why you can eat the same chocolate every day but not your favorite cooked food.

PSYCH TEST **THIS IS WHY YOU STRUGGLE TO PICK A PIZZA**

ANSWER **a. Too many choices incapacitate the brain.** According to psychologists, the menu muddles are caused by choice overload. When the brain is presented with too many similar options, it simply draws a blank.

PSYCH TEST **GIVE YOUR BIASES THE BOOT—AND WIN THIS PRIZE!**

ANSWER **b. Recognizing people and situations for who and what they really are.** Once you uproot your own biases, they cannot cloud your views with assumptions and prejudice. You'll see people and situations more clearly, make better judgment calls, and treat others more fairly.

**PSYCH TEST THE BIAS THAT SEPARATES US**

**ANSWER b. Cherry-picking friends and information to support your own beliefs.** According to psychologists, this bias can be hugely overblown, like an extremist group or, more subtly, like reading only pro-alien reports online to prove your own belief in extraterrestrials.

**PSYCH TEST THE BIAS THAT FOILS YOUR YEARLY RESOLUTIONS**

**ANSWER a. They underestimate how much effort it takes to achieve big goals.** Psychologists believe that most people choose their New Year's goals while under the influence of false hope syndrome. This is characterized by underestimating how much work is needed to accomplish a goal or realize a dream.

**PSYCH TEST WHEN RANDOMNESS LOOKS MEANINGFUL**

**ANSWER a. The clustering illusion.** One example of this happened in World War II. German pilots randomly bombed London, hitting some areas worse than others. British citizens convinced themselves that these "dangerous" locations were chosen for a reason.

**PSYCH TEST THE BRAIN'S VANISHING ACT**

**ANSWER a. By deleting unimportant information, you can focus on what matters.** Researchers believe that by deleting unchanging details, the brain can focus more on important matters. This is why you're mostly unaware of your own nose!

**PSYCH TEST SPEAKING WITH SPOOKS**

**ANSWER b. Auditory hallucinations.** Research indicates that spiritualists experience a controllable and positive auditory hallucinatory process, whereas schizophrenia's "voices" are more uncontrolled and distressing.

**PSYCH TEST UNCONTROLLABLE NIGHTTIME MUNCHIES**

**ANSWER b. Desynchronized circadian rhythm.** Researchers still don't understand how a circadian clock is destabilized, but it's been linked to lower leptin levels (the "full stomach feeling" hormone) and sleepwalking buffets.

**PSYCH TEST THE MISTAKES THAT MORTIFY YOU ARE CUTE**

**ANSWER a. Not being perfect makes you endearing.** According to psychologists, two biases are at play. Feeling that everyone is scrutinizing your mistake (the spotlight effect) and finding flaws relatable (the pratfall effect).

**PSYCH TEST YOU HAVE BUILT-IN PROTECTION AGAINST HALLUCINATIONS**

**ANSWER d. It keeps questioning what it knows.** Psychologists suggest that the brain constantly fact-checks its past beliefs and expectations. When this system fails, it can lead to hallucinations.

**PSYCH TEST THIS BIAS CREATED PLANET NINE (MAYBE)**

ANSWER **a. Selection bias.** According to other astronomers, the original study could've been skewed because of selecting just six objects. This small "sample population" leaves too much room for assumptions.

**PSYCH TEST MORE REASON TO GUZZLE $H_2O$**

ANSWER **a. Lower mood and inability to think clearly.** The University of Connecticut discovered that even mild dehydration can lead to reduced emotional well-being, lower energy levels, and foggy thinking.

**PSYCH TEST PUZZLE OVER THIS**

ANSWER **c. The activity disconnects the brain from daily worries.** According to neuroscientists, the repetitive and calming activity of building a jigsaw puzzle pulls the brain away from daily concerns, basically giving it a break.

**PSYCH TEST THE BRAIN TREATS FOOD AND SOCIALNESS THE SAME**

ANSWER **a. The brain creates cravings for both.** According to scientists, the same pair of brain regions induce powerful cravings for tasty food and social intimacy with loved ones.

**PSYCH TEST THIS BRAIN DIFFERENCE SETS YOUR EMPATHY LEVELS**

ANSWER **b. Mirror neurons.** Research shows that specialized cells called "mirror neurons" are responsible for compassion. Empaths have a hyperactive mirror system, and malignant narcissists have the opposite.

**PSYCH TEST THE BRAIN'S MYSTERIOUS FILTER**

ANSWER **a. It keeps you in the past.** According to some researchers, the brain has a fifteen-second lag behind real time to consolidate all the information it receives into a stable image.

**PSYCH TEST COUNT YOUR MEMORIES!**

ANSWER **c. Seven for thirty seconds.** Studies published in *Psychological Review* suggest that your short-term memory is a tiny room. There's just enough space for seven things. On average, a short-term memory can last between fifteen and thirty seconds.

**PSYCH TEST YOUR EARLIEST MEMORIES—TRUTH OR FICTION?**

ANSWER **d. Your first memories are probably fictitious.** The brain's autobiographical wiring is not fully mature until the age of three or four. Due to this, neurologists seriously doubt that any of your first memories are real.

**PSYCH TEST ANOTHER REASON TO STAND UP STRAIGHT**

ANSWER **b. Improved ability to remember happy memories.** Researchers asked students to slouch and then sit up straight. Both times, they had to recall negative and positive memories. When the students sat up, they recalled more happy memories.

### PSYCH TEST HOW TO CREATE DURABLE MEMORIES

ANSWER **a. Intense feelings, both negative and positive.** The reason why intense emotions create the most vivid, durable memories remains a mystery. But researchers suspect the brain wants you to remember them to both survive and flourish.

### PSYCH TEST REMEMBERING THINGS THAT NEVER HAPPENED

ANSWER **b. Exploring fascinating topics.** During a 2016 study, volunteers viewed news stories (some false) linked to topics they liked and disliked. When questioned, participants "remembered" more false stories when they were connected to their favorite topics.

### PSYCH TEST YOUR MEMORY'S FILING CABINET SYSTEM

ANSWER **b. In connections across the brain.** A 2017 MIT study discovered that memories are initially formed inside the hippocampus but are later stored across the brain, buried inside connections.

### PSYCH TEST GET ARTSY TO EXPERIENCE SUPER MEMORY

ANSWER **b. Doodling or drawing.** The University of Waterloo asked volunteers to copy words by writing the word, then either writing about its attributes or drawing an image of what the word represented. After a break, people recalled more of the doodle-related words.

### PSYCH TEST HOW "BRAINY BOOKMARKS" MAKE LEARNING EASIER

ANSWER **b. Exposure to new things primes the brain to learn about them later on.** According to scientists, when you are exposed to something new, the brain "bookmarks" the experience, making you more ready to learn about the topic in the future.

### PSYCH TEST HOW NEAR-IDENTICAL MEMORIES STAY DIFFERENT

ANSWER **b. Small differences among memories are magnified.** Research has shown that the brain uses memory distortion to separate near-identical memories. The brain exaggerates small details in one memory but not the other, thus making them less similar.

### PSYCH TEST AND THE MOST EFFECTIVE REMINDER IS...?

ANSWER **a. An interesting reminder because it grabs the attention.** Scientists gave customers coupons and told some that a green alien at the counter was a reminder to use it. Those who had been told this used their cards more often than those who didn't. Boring reminders don't have the same effect.

### PSYCH TEST ELDERLY FORGETFULNESS IS NOT WHAT YOU THINK

ANSWER **c. Taking in too much information.** Researchers found that older adults tend to absorb more details when learning something new. Ironically, cluttering their brain with details prevents durable memories.

PSYCH TEST **YOU MIGHT NOT BE REAL**

ANSWER **a. You create false memories to fit your identity.** Researchers found that you forge false memories that reinforce your identity—and selectively recall real memories that do the same. This process is mostly subconscious.

PSYCH TEST **HOW FULL IS YOUR BRAIN?**

ANSWER **c. Old information is pushed out.** Behavioral studies published in *Nature Neurostudies* show that the brain compares similar things and discards older, unused information. For example, it forgets an old PIN for a new one.

PSYCH TEST **COMBAT AND MEMORY**

ANSWER **b. One minute.** Researchers at the University of Portsmouth found that it takes sixty seconds to damage the memories of police officers in threatening situations that require physical combat.

PSYCH TEST **TRY THIS FUN MEMORY AID**

ANSWER **c. Talking to another person.** Amazingly, researchers published a study in *Social Psychological and Personality Science* stating that it takes just ten minutes of conversation with someone to improve your cognitive functioning, memory, and test scores.

PSYCH TEST **MEMORIES CAN HELP WITH PANIC ATTACKS**

ANSWER **b. Recalling a completely accepting friend.** Research shows that the thought of a friend who is physically and emotionally safe can calm one's parasympathetic nervous system, where panic originates.

PSYCH TEST **HOW TO SACRIFICE MEMORY FOR MEMORY**

ANSWER **a. Repetition learning.** This cornerstone of education helps students to absorb tons of information. But researchers found that memories created in this way keep losing details over time.

PSYCH TEST **THE STRANGE WAY YOU REMEMBER**

ANSWER **a. The brain reverses the process.** According to scientists, when you remember something that you saw, the brain first pulls up the context and then adds smaller details about the object.

PSYCH TEST **SUGAR CAN SHOCK YOUR MEMORY**

ANSWER **c. It disrupts connections in the hippocampus.** Research indicates that during septic shock, sugar enters the bloodstream. Sometimes, it leaks into the brain's hippocampus and interferes with circuits related to memory.

PSYCH TEST **OLD MEMORIES LEAVE ECHOES**

ANSWER **a. Only the most important part, or "gist."** The universities of Glasgow and Birmingham demonstrated that memories eventually lose their details but not their core. For example, you remember a particularly tasty lunch but not your outfit.

**PSYCH TEST SKIP THE URGE TO COMFORT-SMILE**

ANSWER **a. Reduced well-being and a lower-quality bond with the child.** Researchers found that parents who hide problems from their kids, especially behind a happy smile, feel so bad afterward that they experience a lower sense of well-being and a weaker parent-child bond.

**PSYCH TEST THERE ARE TWO GREEN-EYED MONSTERS**

ANSWER **c. A perceived threat to something you value, real or imagined.** Jealousy happens when a third party threatens a valuable bond, whether it's romantic or vying for the boss's approval. Envy involves two people, one of whom wants what the other one has.

**PSYCH TEST TEARS ARE NATURAL TRANQUILIZERS**

ANSWER **c. It gets rid of stress hormones while also releasing feel-good hormones.** This biological process is designed to balance the body after you experience overwhelming emotions. Crying expels stress hormones and floods the system with endorphins, which act as painkillers and tranquilizers.

**PSYCH TEST THE BRIGHT SIDE OF DISGUST**

ANSWER **a. It keeps you safe from potentially dangerous things.** When a university exposed students to dirty tiles, disgust-prone participants were better at detecting smaller specks of dirt. This suggests that revulsion helps you to avoid unseen dangers like germs.

**PSYCH TEST THE LIFE SPAN OF EMOTIONS**

ANSWER **d. Ninety seconds.** The biochemical process behind emotions takes ninety seconds from activation to flushing the chemicals from the body. If you keep stimulating an emotion, the process loops as a single, longer experience.

**PSYCH TEST NEW GRANDPARENTS PLUCK THIS NERVE**

ANSWER **a. Loving their child reminds parents of the missing love in their own childhood.** According to psychologists, when new parents feel deeply protective of their newborn, they can become resentful of their own parents, who didn't show them the same care and protection.

**PSYCH TEST WHAT REALLY MAKES BUSY BEES HAPPY**

ANSWER **c. Enjoying tasks that are meaningful.** It doesn't matter what financial reward awaits or how much support you receive: Meaningless work is soul-crushing. Psychologists believe people are happiest when they're busy with enjoyable, worthwhile tasks.

PSYCH TEST **WHEN YOU'RE MORE THAN HOMESICK**

ANSWER **c. You are mentally and emotionally trapped in your past.** Studies involving expats and refugees indicate that leaving behind something emotional, like a sense of safety, family, or belonging, can prevent people from moving forward.

PSYCH TEST **WHY FRIEND BREAKUPS HIT LIKE A HAMMER**

ANSWER **a. It triggers disenfranchised grief.** Psychologists suggest that with friend breakups, people experience disenfranchised grief (a loss others don't see as legitimate), leaving them without the support they need to heal.

PSYCH TEST **WHEN THE CALMNESS IS CALLOUS**

ANSWER **a. Turning one's focus inward is unsettling.** Researchers believe that the main cause of paradoxical anxiety is swapping the busy, distracting world for inner quiet. This can be unnerving for some.

PSYCH TEST **MEET YOUR FIRST FEELINGS**

ANSWER **c. Nine.** According to some researchers, your primary affects are enjoyment, interest, surprise, distress, fear, anger, shame, disgust for bad tastes, and a revulsion of noxious smells.

PSYCH TEST **A FRIEND TRACTOR BEAM**

ANSWER **a. Gratitude.** Studies indicate that gratitude is a positive signal and that people are more likely to form relationships with those who have expressed thanks in the past.

PSYCH TEST **THIS LIGHT AMPS UP YOUR EMOTIONS!**

ANSWER **c. Bright light.** According to scientists, bright light can intensify your mood and affect how you make decisions. Low light can do the opposite.

PSYCH TEST **FOLLOW THE VOICE**

ANSWER **c. You adjust your mood to match the emotions in your voice.** French researchers have discovered that your voice reflects what you're really feeling and that you subconsciously adjust your mood to these emotions.

PSYCH TEST **THIS EMOTION IS A LONG-DISTANCE RUNNER**

ANSWER **c. Sadness.** When researchers at KU Leuven studied the durability of feelings, they found that sadness can endure up to 240 times longer than other emotions.

PSYCH TEST **ARE YOU GUILTY OF GUILT?**

ANSWER **c. Five.** Research indicates that when you add up all the minutes you spend feeling guilty, it equals roughly five hours a week.

PSYCH TEST **AN EMOTIONAL POTION FOR WISDOM**

ANSWER **a. Emotional control, empathy, and curiosity.** Although wisdom is a complex thing, experts agree that concern for others, open-minded curiosity, and regulating one's emotions all contribute to your Zen factor!

### PSYCH TEST **EMPLOYEES GONE WILD**

ANSWER **a. More rule-breaking and resentment.** Research shows that tracking doesn't always keep employees in line. A lot of workers break more rules because of resentment and feelings of diminished responsibility.

### PSYCH TEST **THE WONDER OF AWE**

ANSWER **b. It calms and refreshes the mind.** According to experts, a moment of awe has the power to calm anxiety, refresh your mind, and leave you with a sense of well-being.

## CHAPTER 6

### PSYCH TEST **THIS SILVER LINING HAS A DARK CLOUD**

ANSWER **b. A deep sense of guilt.** Individuals with empathy often feel like they have to erase the suffering of others. Since this is not always possible, it can lead to feelings of despair, guilt, and even depression.

### PSYCH TEST **A SIMPLE SKILL THAT FOILS PSYCHOPATHS**

ANSWER **a. Recognize facial expressions.** Research has indicated that people with antisocial disorders have trouble recognizing expressions. A psychopath's brain has almost no reaction to a fearful face, which may explain why they lack remorse for their violent actions.

### PSYCH TEST **SOMETIMES IT'S BEST TO NOT THINK**

ANSWER **a. Struggling to communicate coherent thoughts and speech.** A thought disorder can be exceptionally hard to diagnose, but psychologists often recognize the signs when a person struggles to write, speak, or think coherently.

### PSYCH TEST **SOME EMPATHS ARE CREEPY TOO**

ANSWER **b. The ability to recognize and manipulate someone's emotions.** According to psychologists, dark empaths can, like their benevolent counterparts, also sense other people's feelings and needs. However, they use this to their own advantage, usually by manipulating someone's emotions.

### PSYCH TEST **WHY DEPRESSION ERASES COLORS**

ANSWER **a. Depression slows retinal response to color contrasts.** A small study in 2010 discovered that depression can lower your retinal response to the contrasts between colors. This might explain why affected individuals cannot see colors the normal way.

### PSYCH TEST **CAN YOU DO ME ANOTHER FAVOR?**

ANSWER **a. The foot-in-the-door technique.** Psychologists believe this technique is so powerful because people hesitate to refuse a larger favor when they have already agreed to a smaller, related request.

---

PSYCH TEST **WATCH OUT FOR THIS WEATHER!**

ANSWER **b. Cloudy weather.** During a 2014 study, dark triad individuals approached people on the street. On cloudy days, the Machiavellians' confidence and social acceptance outstripped the narcissists and psychopaths.

---

PSYCH TEST **911? YEAH, I'M GUILTY...**

ANSWER **c. Murderers are more theatrical and less forthright.** An extensive study by researchers at Villanova University found that killers who place 911 calls are less candid, helpful, or cooperative. They also tend to be highly emotional and dramatic.

---

PSYCH TEST **WHY ARE YOU SO *QUIET*?**

ANSWER **b. Mocking or bullying an individual for staying in the background.** Introverts are often shamed for avoiding the limelight. According to psychiatrists, such pressure to be more extroverted just causes more social anxiety for introverts.

---

PSYCH TEST **WHEN OLDER SIBLINGS SIN**

ANSWER **d. A greater risk of following in their footsteps.** Two university studies found that younger siblings close in age to the offending sibling run a greater risk of committing a violent criminal act themselves.

PSYCH TEST **PUNISHING A PSYCHOPATH IS...COMPLICATED**

ANSWER **b. Their brains do not understand punishment.** An MRI study by researchers in Canada and the UK found that violent psychopathic offenders have brain abnormalities that hamper normal functions. One of these regions controls learning from punishment.

---

PSYCH TEST **ONLY THE NARCISSIST CAN SHINE**

ANSWER **a. Minimizing the achievements.** According to psychologists, the narcissist's core desire to stand at the center of everything makes them belittle others, especially when they accomplish great things.

---

PSYCH TEST **NEGATIVE BROWNIE POINTS**

ANSWER **b. After doing someone a favor, they milk it for months.** Psychologists view this as a classic manipulation method. Abusers gain power over others by reminding them of all the good things they've done for them.

---

PSYCH TEST **I'M IGNORING YOU**

ANSWER **c. It punishes, hurts, and manipulates a partner.** In psychology, the "silent treatment" is considered an insidious way to control a partner by refusing to acknowledge them or talk to them.

---

PSYCH TEST **DOING BUSINESS WITH THE DARK TRIAD? TRY THIS!**

ANSWER **a. Communicate with them online.** Research shows that dark triad individuals, who are usually silver-tongued, struggle to portray themselves as sincere or to manipulate others when they use online chat platforms.

PSYCH TEST **TWO JERKS IN A ROOM...**

ANSWER **b. A high chance of a successful meeting.** Studies from the University of Georgia showed that when people with similar personalities meet, even if they are both jerks, they have more successful negotiations than those without.

PSYCH TEST **A LEAFY INFLUENCE ON LAWBREAKERS**

ANSWER **b. Reduced property damage and violent crimes.** A Portland study found that lots with large trees had less damage and crimes, possibly because thieves thought the properties were better cared for and protected.

PSYCH TEST **HOW TO SPOT A FUGITIVE 101**

ANSWER **b. Real fugitives are exceptionally boring people.** Crime research shows that smart fugitives present themselves as boring and forgettable. This allows them to blend in and fool others, sometimes for years.

PSYCH TEST **TOO MUCH OF A BAD THING**

ANSWER **c. Too much lead in the environment.** During a population study, Australian researchers found a strong link between children who'd endured long exposure to environmental lead and aggressive crime in later life.

PSYCH TEST **YOU CAN BLAME THE PARENTS FOR THIS ONE**

ANSWER **a. Giving their child an unpopular name.** According to an article in *Social Science Quarterly*, when an adolescent's name is considered dull or unpopular, it could be a factor in unruly behavior, probably because of bullying or because they dislike their name.

PSYCH TEST **YOUR BRAIN IS A NIGHTTIME NAG**

ANSWER **c. It's a survival strategy.** Some psychologists believe that bedtime regret is a survival mechanism that uses emotional pain to ensure that you avoid similar situations in the future.

PSYCH TEST **WHY GROUPS AREN'T GOOD IN A CRISIS**

ANSWER **c. Rumors, group safety, and denial can delay action.** When researchers asked groups to decide whether they should evacuate a hypothetical disaster, critical evacuations were delayed because people denied the danger in favor of positive rumors and group security.

PSYCH TEST **HEY YOU!**

ANSWER **a. You recognize their body language.** Research indicates that you excel at recognizing a friend's body language long before you see their face, even when you're not consciously trying to do so.

PSYCH TEST **ARE THE WEALTHY REALLY SO SNOOTY?**

ANSWER **c. Upper-class culture has less motivation to look at faces.** Research indicates that very wealthy individuals often ignore passersby because they're raised to believe that lower social groups aren't a threat, meaning that they have less motivation to assess strangers.

PSYCH TEST **WE'RE ALL A BUNCH OF COPYCATS**

ANSWER **a. To build rapport with the person being mimicked.** In psychology, positive mirroring happens subconsciously when you like someone. Negative mirroring is an intentional manipulation tactic. Either way, the goal is to create a rapport with the person being copied.

PSYCH TEST **THE LURE OF LUCKY LOTTO NUMBERS**

ANSWER **c. They fear their numbers will be drawn should they not play.** According to psychologists, lottery fans play the same numbers because it "increases" their chance of being drawn. This illusion also convinces people that they genuinely risk losing millions if they don't play.

PSYCH TEST **SHOPPING WITHOUT A VIEW**

ANSWER **c. Undistracted customers stay in the store for longer.** According to experts, supermarkets don't have windows because they want you to zone out from the real world and focus solely on shopping (and hopefully buy more).

PSYCH TEST **IT'S GOOD TO STARE AT YOUR SPOUSE**

ANSWER **a. Deeper feelings of marital satisfaction.** Researchers found that people who look at photos of their spouse experience deeper feelings of attachment, infatuation, and more satisfaction with their marriage.

PSYCH TEST **LET'S STAMPEDE THIS WAY**

ANSWER **b. Just 5 percent.** Remarkably, researchers discovered that herd mentality makes 95 percent of people snake after the 5 percent without knowing why or where they're headed.

PSYCH TEST **WE ALL HAVE FRIEND BLINDNESS**

ANSWER **c. You might misjudge how poorly they're performing on a task.** According to psychologists, you view friends more positively than strangers. This can cause oversights during performance checks or job interviews, or when friends make mistakes.

PSYCH TEST **LET'S DISCUSS THAT CULT LEADER**

ANSWER **b. Malignant narcissist.** Although rare exceptions exist, experts believe that most cult leaders are malignant narcissists, a particularly toxic dark triad personality.

PSYCH TEST **HAPPY COUPLES QUARREL DIFFERENTLY**

ANSWER **a. Topics that can be resolved.** A study performed by the University of Tennessee found that couples are happier with their marriage when they avoid conflicts that can never be fully resolved, like in-laws or religion.

### PSYCH TEST **BEAUTY'S SOCIAL FACTOR**

ANSWER **c. The attractiveness of those around the person.** Research shows that, in a crowd, you judge how good-looking someone is by looking at the attractiveness of the people around them.

### PSYCH TEST **THE BASIC GOODS TRICK**

ANSWER **c. Customers have to walk past other products, causing impulse buys.** Research shows that when customers have to walk to the back of a store, they pass a maximum number of other products, and this leads to spontaneous purchases.

### PSYCH TEST **HOW SHUNNED GROUPS KICK PREJUDICE TO THE CURB**

ANSWER **a. They modify their behavior to prove the assumptions wrong.** Research shows that victims of stereotyping sometimes put their best foot forward. Overweight individuals might dress neatly to counter some people's assumption that the obese are unkempt.

### PSYCH TEST **DEAR SHOPPER, WE MAKE YOU FEEL RICH**

ANSWER **c. Play calm or classical music.** Commercial research indicates that you associate classical tunes and calm music with wealth. The underlying feeling of privilege makes shoppers relax their resistance to spending!

### PSYCH TEST **WHEN FOOTBALL FANS WATCH REPLAY ADS**

ANSWER **c. Fans who like the replays like the brand.** Research indicates that when replays highlight one team's success in any way, their fans are more likely to positively glom on to the advertised brand.

### PSYCH TEST **READY, SET...SHOP!**

ANSWER **b. They bargain hunt when they can afford the full price.** Researchers define sport shoppers as people who love the thrill of outsmarting the retail system by securing a bargain when they can pay the full price.

### PSYCH TEST **THIS SUCKS BUT I DON'T WANT TO BREAK UP**

ANSWER **a. They feel that leaving will be bad for their partner.** A study published in the *Journal of Personality and Social Psychology* found that the more someone feels that their partner is emotionally dependent on them, the less likely they are to leave.

### PSYCH TEST **TRUST MAKES YOU A LITTLE DELUSIONAL**

ANSWER **c. Forgetting small transgressions leads to a healthier relationship.** Researchers found that trust can cast memories of a romantic partner's small transgressions in a more positive light, or even erase them completely. This can be beneficial for some couples.

# INDEX

## E



## F



## G



## H



## I

## S



## T



## U



## V



## W



## Z